PROMOTION AND TENURE CONFIDENTIAL

# PROMOTION AND TENURE CONFIDENTIAL

✦

DAVID D. PERLMUTTER

Harvard University Press
Cambridge, Massachusetts
London, England
2010

*Library of Congress Cataloging-in-Publication Data*

Perlmutter, David D., 1962–
Promotion and tenure confidential / David D. Perlmutter.
p.   cm.
Includes bibliographical references and index.
ISBN 978-0-674-04878-2 (alk. paper)
1. College teachers—Tenure—United States.   2. College teachers—Promotions—United
States.   3. College teaching—Vocational guidance—United States.   I. Title.
LB2335.7.P47   2010
378.1'214—dc22       2010014756

*To my wife, Christie, without whose help, counsel, and sympathy this book would not have been possible.*

# Contents

Derive happiness in oneself from a good day's work, from illuminating the fog that surrounds us.

—*Henri Matisse*

# Introduction:
# Promotion and Tenure Up Close
# and Personal

❋

Years ago a brilliant young tenure-track mathematician described to me the thorniest issues he confronted in his pursuit to becoming a tenured associate professor. Instead of bemoaning difficulties with his equations or advancing theory, he lamented that his post-doc assistant was not completing vital tasks on time and was seriously delaying their joint project, his department chair held an ethic of avoiding work at all costs and so discouraged junior faculty from obtaining grants, and a senior professor was throwing eye daggers at him during faculty meetings for no fathomable reason. Everything considered, the young scholar felt he could handle the intellectual labors of being an academic but was confused and oppressed by the human relations and political challenges. After I put forward some plausible explanations for the behaviors of his problem colleagues, the younger man asked, "Why didn't they offer a course in 'Being a Professor 101' in graduate school?"

Why not, indeed? Most academic disciplines adequately train graduate students in conducting research and do a fair job in tutoring them how to teach but do a poor job in inculcating in them the skills and ethos to become satisfied and successful *tenured professors*. As Brown University history professor Evelyn Hu-DeHart recalled:

> Among the many things we never learned about in graduate school, one matter concerns what might be termed 'office politics' among

the faculty. Oh, to be sure, we heard bits and pieces of gossip about faculty relationships and interactions, but as graduate students, we were rarely ever privy to what really went on behind those closed doors during departmental meetings or in the chair's office.[1]

My response is *Promotion and Tenure Confidential,* a synthesis of research, interviews, consultations, and personal experiences about surviving and prospering in academia. In these pages I try to reveal as critically and as candidly as possible the "behind closed doors" and "people-incited" events, issues, processes, and relations that affect victory or failure in our singular profession.

My perspective, I will admit, is not clinical and disengaged. Both of my parents were professors; I first heard about a "tenure vote" around the age when I was learning to ride a bike. Over the intervening years, and through grad school, I became more intrigued with this mysterious procedure. How and why did people negotiate the process? Was it a matter of luck, skill, intelligence, scheming, or a mixture of all these? Were there underlying patterns or theories of promotion and tenure (P&T)? Could one develop a philosophy about the enterprise of becoming a tenured professor?

By now I feel that P&T is (a) worthy of exploration on an intellectual and practical basis, (b) full of intricacies and subtleties, (c) a veritable field laboratory of human behavior, and (d) sadly, an experience that leaves many of us feeling battered and wounded, whether we win or not.

After I received tenure myself, I began writing for the *Chronicle of Higher Education,* at first intermittently and then monthly, in a column called "P&T Confidential." By e-mail, on the phone, and at faculty functions, conventions, and assorted water holes of academia, I listened to tenure trackers lament and laugh about their adventures, tragic, triumphant, and comic. (I once missed a flight connection because I was absorbed in the story of a young biologist who was convinced that a colleague had tampered with the food of her lab rats.)

From these sources and evidence, I generated some basic principles about academic careers.

## Academic Careers Can Be Planned (in Part)

The more I heard and read about P&T, the more convinced I was that reaching a secure position in the professoriate is not a matter of following "five secrets" or "ten tips" or a dozen aphorisms. Given all the different types of institutions, one set of advice cannot fit all. But anyone seeking P&T (and then another promotion!) should be aware of the common body of research, experiences, and observations that will lessen the chances of stumbling in the career ascent.

So, unless you believe in divine predestination, you probably agree that life contains some factors that are controlled by external actors, ranging from fellow humans to nature, while other factors are affected by luck or random chance; yet there are still more factors over which you have some power. "Control" implies forethought, a belief that the future can be at least to some extent anticipated and planned for. Perhaps illogically, though, many academics engage in little career planning. We seem to hold the theory that we should hold no theory about how to achieve career success. The reasons for this ostrich-mindedness about our own vocation are complicated.

First, surely we professors like to think that we are different from (read: superior to) other professionals. Let the insurance agents and used-car hawkers peruse books on being a super sales whiz. What academic would be caught reading *Pedagogy for Dummies* in the faculty club? Or mention to colleagues that she paid to attend a seminar entitled *Be a Top Scholar in Ten Days without Really Trying!* Or tell the head of the P&T committee that her tenure bid's chances are improved because she saw an inspirational video on *Chicken Soup for the Scientist's Soul?*

Planning out a professorial career seems Machiavellian as well as undignified. As one young assistant professor asked me, "Shouldn't I just be good and be rewarded for it?" He added, "If I focus too much on a career plan, doesn't that make me a schemer?" My answer: You plan and plot your research, your courses, even your summer vacation—why not your career? Furthermore, "good" must include not only research and teaching but understanding the three Ps of P&T: the people and politics and personal conundrums of our business. There is no conflict between career advancement and virtue: You can be a *good*—that is decent, caring, and ethical—professor as well as a tenured one.

Ego is a factor as well. In certifying someone a "doctor" of philosophy or science, you knight them to be among the best and brightest in an area of study. How can you follow up with the warning that their knowledge of human relations and office politics may be at the elementary-school level? I have seen, learned of, and heard from not a few tenure trackers who are probably geniuses in their fields but naïve to the point of self-destruction in their careers. Getting good advice about P&T, or even being seen reading a book about it, is not an admission of a lack of intellect any more than reading a new journal article on a research topic is an embarrassing declaration of ignorance.

Another basis for avoiding P&T as a topic is an understandable ethic not to embarrass ourselves in front of the juniors. Many of us in academia do not want to drag graduate students into our petty political battles, personal tiffs, power plays, and minor scandals. Most academics would prefer to maintain that success in our business is all a matter of intelligence, creativity, and industry. To be sure, those traits are supremely useful. Foolishness, insipidity, and lax teaching and scholarship habits are career-killers, and rightly so. But if you are incapable of understanding the human relationships, politics, sociology, psychology, and managerial insights of being an academic, you are pursuing your dream of advancement in our business with severe handicaps.

Although all sorts of obstacles and opportunities will pop up, many of them are, in fact, foreseeable or reckoned as possible, and any good plan will anticipate or prepare for crises and contingencies. I see an analogy from my own research conducted during an ethnography of police work.[2] Cops and trainers for seminars in how to avoid being a crime victim give similar advice: rehearse so that you won't be surprised. So, for example, in a typical antivictimhood workshop, you will be asked to think about what you would do if someone jumped you while you were opening your car door in a parking lot. Would you fight, scream for help, or comply with any threats and demands? The analogy is a grim one, I admit, but I likewise think the young academic should know what kind of political and people threats and opportunities she *might* face on the P&T track so that she can weigh an appropriate response and is neither stunned into paralysis nor reacts viscerally without estimation of consequences.

Take the story of an assistant professor denied tenure despite what appeared to be an outstanding record of research, teaching, and service. He found out that one of the reasons the higher university administration had nixed his bid was the influence of a senior faculty member in his unit. This fine fellow had been Chaucer's proverbial "smyler with the knyfe under the cloke." Feigning to be helpful, even a mentor, the senior professor had been a font of bad advice and a source of consistent backstabbing, all the while remaining genial and collegial in outward manner. Why? My suspicion is that the young man's precociousness in research, teaching, and service *in the identical subfield as the old man* sank him; the latter, following the path of envy, ego, and insecurity, wanted no competition for glory, grants, or prestige within the same school.

As in many stories in this book, my sources are singular and limited. I don't claim—barring a legal investigation—to know the whole truth. The point is, his "story" was illustrative of cases that do occur. This devilish situation illustrates that not all dilemmas on the tenure track have ready-made or cookie-cutter solutions. In the chapters to come I will suggest ways to deal with problem people. I will make the case that even the most malevolent antagonist may, if for no other reason than self-interest, be willing to negotiate a deal with you and end up supporting your job candidacy or your tenure bid or at least not sabotaging it.

But sometimes failure is unavoidable. You can figure out the game, play by the rules, and still not seize the prize because of the perfidy of the other players or even the referees. I still maintain, however, that at least thinking through the possible scenarios that you will encounter on your odyssey is better than stumbling into them blindly. *Promotion and Tenure Confidential* does not feign that you can "self-help" your way out of every difficulty, but it will identify and offer some possible ameliorative tactics for the most common three-P troubles.

## An Academic Career Is a Personal Odyssey

The career paths of academics are marked by bureaucratic decisions made within large organizations with systems, rules, bylaws, protocols, and legal codes. But those who have nibbled their fingernails waiting to hear about a P&T committee vote can testify that success and happiness in our profession are also dependent on the beliefs, whims, and moods of *people*. Yes, hiring and P&T decisions are data-driven to some degree, but your character, your behavior, your personality, and the feelings and emotions you engender in colleagues, students, administrators, and external peers are part of the evidence upon which hiring and P&T committees and deans will base their judgments.

Although your career in academia is not "all about you," you are obviously the primary influence over your own destiny. I recall the observation of Raymond Strother, the legendary political consultant: in a campaign the most important message is the candidate himself. Academia has its team elements; those who fail to pitch in will be hurt on practically every rung of the career ladder (and may even get shaken off it).[3] Still, the solo aspects of our trade are vital. Whether you are one of twenty doctoral assistants in a large chemistry laboratory at a research university working on a huge collaborative grant project, or an assistant professor of Romance languages at a liberal arts college trying to finish your first book before the tenure clock runs out, or an associate professor at a community college designing your lesson plans for a new prep, at the end of the day you stand alone. Others can hinder or help, but your decisions about your own career will have the greatest impact on it. Knowing yourself is the first step to controlling your future.[4]

But self-reflecting on our own character and characteristics is not a normal human activity, not even for people who make it their business to understand natural or human phenomena. Professors in psychology—or physics or botany or German—are not immune to the cognitive and behavioral mechanisms that govern the sophomores in psych experiments. To use one example that has strong tenure-track effects, all members of our species have a predilection for "feedback that fits":[5] we prefer data that reinforce our existing beliefs (or that we have interpreted to do so). In my own field of visual/political communication, we call this the "believing is seeing" tendency.[6] Just because such a modality of thinking is natural, however, does not make it functional when you are trying to finish your dissertation and must absorb the constructive and accurate but painful criticism your committee has offered of the first draft.

*Promotion and Tenure Confidential* is written, in part, because I have seen too many great minds and souls sabotage their own careers, most likely without conscious knowledge of their mistakes. To quote Mike Tyson, "I never lost a fight to another fighter, but I lost plenty to myself."[7]

## Promotion and Tenure Are Getting Harder and Rarer

Tenure counts: the number of full-time, tenured faculty who are individually terminated each year is so small that when it happens it is newsworthy. Because schools rarely publish these data, only approximations can be made, but according to the American Association of University Professors, "About 50 faculty members lose their tenured position for cause each year."[8] In 1991, when the University of California dismissed a tenured associate professor, the event was reported to be a first "in the 123-year history of the nine-campus [UC system]."[9]

That is not to say that tenure will continue to be a general protection from unemployment. At the time of the writing of this book in 2010, wholesale elimination of academic departments and firing of their tenured professors (so-called vertical cuts) made the news in several high-profile cases. We can only hope that such layoffs, unfortunately familiar to the business and industrial world, will not become common in our profession, but it is always a possibility in bad economic times. Equally ominous were more and more instances of alleged "economic denial" of tenure. An assistant professor meets or exceeds the P&T criteria of her institution, wins the unanimous vote of her faculty, receives ringing endorsements from outside evaluators, and then is turned down by upper administration. The suspected reason: the college or university simply does not want someone on the payroll teaching some esoteric subfield for another forty years. Why not just hire cheaper contingent faculty at will?

At the same time the tenured professor is becoming a rare (or rarer) bird—not quantitatively, but relative to other kinds of faculty.[10] By some counts, as of 2007 only 21.3 percent of America's higher educators were full-time, tenured faculty, down from 36.5 percent in 1975.[11] The travails of adjuncts, teaching single courses at many schools, struggling to gas up the car for long commutes and receiving inadequate medical insurance, are frequent topics of lament in faculty publications and blogs. Certainly, forbidding to assistant professors is the specter of becoming a "scholar-gypsy" after being denied tenure.[12] Most revealing of all, many political and administrative leaders (and a few professors) would like to junk the system entirely. A 2005 survey of presidents of four-year colleges found that over half of them wanted to replace tenure with long-term contracts.[13]

The pressure to get tenure, then, is felt deeply for good reason. Although denial of tenure is not the end of a career, the safety net of other positions grows smaller. No surprise that voluminous research has found that the quest for tenure is a significant source of stress in the lives of assistant professors.[14] As one young tenure tracker put it, "It's like you know that on a certain date, a few years down the road, people will vote on whether you live or die." It can certainly seem that way, and to paraphrase Dr. Johnson, nothing so focuses the mind as the prospect of being executed—even if it is six years in the future.

Yet the new Ph.D. has already survived a considerable winnowing.[15] About half of doctoral students will drop out before graduating. An astounding 50 percent of humanities doctoral students have not finished their dissertations after ten years in a program. One scholar, recounting his own experience, stated, "Any graduate program in English is a veritable scrap-yard of dashed hopes, staggering triumphs, misplaced anxieties, bizarre daddy-relationships, and burnouts."[16]

Nevertheless, the products of this pipeline truly are the best and the brightest in terms of academic achievement and potential, perhaps in the entire history of education. The competition for spots in top doctoral programs, the rigors involved in writing a modern dissertation, and the climbing bar of P&T have yielded a population of doctoral students and young faculty who are indeed, to paraphrase Garrison Keillor's description of the youth of Lake Wobegon, all "above average."

That some don't get tenure, that others drop out of the track altogether, angry and embittered, is a waste of resources, time, and above all, people. *Promotion and Tenure Confidential*, however, is not a reform tract. Yes, we should all try our best to improve both the process and the number of tenure track, as opposed to adjunct, positions. But we also need to help people survive within the system as it now exists. It is more helpful for your career and your mental stability to identify the positive ways you can plan to achieve tenure than to dwell on its angst, unfairness, absurdities, and indignities. Work for change; deal with reality.

## Academic Careers Are (or Should Be) Balanced by Our "Other" Lives

At one university in which I taught, some fifteen years ago, a female colleague visited the human resources department to review the maternity policy. She was told that there was maternity leave for staff but not for faculty because it was assumed teachers would have their babies during the summer.[17] Fewer such surreal conversations are taking place now, but the fact is that the academic world has been very slow to recognize that professors have any life outside of their work.

Faculty perceptions of the college life and workplace have probably been studied more thoroughly in the last thirty years than in the previous three hundred.[18] Underlying this interest in ourselves are the changing demographics and psychographics of the academy that demand a holistic, or whole body-mind-spirit, approach to successful P&T. Forty years ago, an advice book for higher education faculty careers could have been written on the assumption that the work life and the workplace were the be-all and end-all of academe. The audience was reasonably homogenous: white males in their thirties and forties whose wives worked at home or in a clerical or service job.

Things have changed, although we are not as diverse as we could be. The National Center for Educational Statistics reported that in the year 2000 about 82 percent of people who earned a doctoral degree were white,[19] and in 2003 whites (47 percent male, 36 percent female) made up 83 percent of the existing faculty.[20] At the same time, people from many ethnic backgrounds and races (as well as gays and lesbians no longer in the closet) are entering the profession, often with particular needs, wants, expectations, and mindsets. In the humanities, social sciences, and life sciences, for example, more women get their doctorates each year than do men.[21] Many studies testify to the tension female academics experience in balancing careers and home lives, especially when raising children.[22] Tenure-track women report greater feelings of being torn between home and the office than do tenure-track men. In fact, the metaphor of balancing on a tightrope, physically and mentally, is a common description of the "mommy on the tenure track." Janice Witherspoon Neuleib, a professor of English at Illinois State University, in an essay on the challenges women face in their personnel reviews, wrote, "The required trick [for getting tenure] which one of my young probationary friends seems to be carrying off, is to speak boldly but with reserve, walk the halls unobtrusively although she is eight months pregnant, and publish madly with a two-year-old helping out at the computer."[23] That's some deft prestidigitation and acrobatics, and many tenure-track women resent the Houdini- and Wallenda-like demands placed on them at the office and at home.

Today's younger academics also ask more of their job as a function of life. Whereas in my father's day a young man would be bluntly told by a senior mentor, "Let your wife take care of everything at home; all your focus must be on research," nowadays junior professors, both male and female, want a happy and fulfilled life, intellectually and in the office and home. They don't expect to have it all—usually—but they do want, as one young colleague put it, "to be my daughter's Brownie troop leader, to go on vacations, and to get tenure." The university is the site of a perfect storm of individual expectations and impersonal bureaucracy, and P&T is the clashing point.

## After Note: How to Read This Book

Some texts, such as murder mysteries and toy assembly instructions, are meant to be read linearly. You must begin at point A and proceed, step by step, to Z. Readers of this book, in contrast, may find themselves at varying stages of the tenure track or may have different interests at any given moment. You may feel you have teaching covered but are considering leaving one tenure-track job for another, or perhaps you find supervising graduate assistants challenging. Many sections, therefore, are self-contained. Feel free to skip around.

That said, there are crossovers in any attempt at covering the major aspects of academic careers. Advice about getting along with (but not being exploited by) your advisers in a doctoral program is equally applicable to the same issues and concerns for the probationary faculty member on her third year on "the track." And as a young tenure tracker facing being a doctoral adviser yourself for the first time, you might want to consider what the students need from you.

So as not to repeat myself too often I have tried to concentrate the appropriate discussions where they make the most sense but in other places introduce or recap the key points. For example, in the chapter on the doctoral years I briefly mention time management, but the lengthy focus on that all-important subject comes later.

I also don't try to encompass everything in higher education that affects your career. There are many fine books and articles, for instance, on teaching in the humanities, or on research in the sciences. You should read such wisdom especially as relates to your own field and institutional situation, such as teaching biology in a community college, French at a small liberal arts college, or architecture at a high-research university. *Promotion and Tenure Confidential* is meant to complement that literature, not supersede it or offer tricks to avoid being a good teacher or researcher altogether. I restrict myself to those aspects of the early academic career, the doctoral years through the tenure track, that influence and are influenced by *human and political factors*.

In addition, this book will notably not follow the advice from the refrain of the Johnny Mercer song "Ac-cent-tchu-ate the Positive." I will talk about negatives, offer horror stories, and lay out frightening scenarios; all are possible occurrences in doctoral programs, job hunting, and the tenure track. Many people pass through to associate professor with few of them actually happening, but if I am overly grim here it is because one bad apple can literally spoil the barrel. A truly dysfunctional three-P offender, victim, or crisis can unravel a heretofore successful career ascent. My goal is not to strike fear but to inoculate. My solutions, in contrast, will be positive: what you can do to help yourself.

Finally, this is not meant to be a special-case book, nor is it written at a granular level of inspection. Although the older, tenure-track African American psychologist at a regional state university, the lesbian graduate student in a small religious college, and the single-parent biology post-doc at a high-research public flagship university may confront particular P&T challenges, I address the issues that cut across race, ethnicity, creed, sex, institutional size and type, and field. I offer here, thus, a survey of the three Ps of P&T, that is, the common people, politics, and personal problems that potentially anyone—black or white, male or female, physical scientist or humanities scholar—might face on the tenure track and beyond.

# CHAPTER 1

# The Doctorate and the Career Track

The tenure track, most people agree today, unofficially begins in graduate school. The groundwork, however, might be laid in the womb. A classic study of the American academic profession[1] found that professors

- tended to view problems as intellectual challenges.
- had a sense of "apartness" that allowed them to work alone.
- preferred activities that could be accomplished autonomously with minimal supervision.
- came from an only- or two-child household.
- grew up in an intellectually stimulating environment.

The "class" factor is formative as well: Melanie R. Benson, a Native American Studies scholar, recounted how discouraging and envy-producing it was to attend graduate school with people mostly from upper-middle and upper-class backgrounds while she came from poverty and survived by "scouring bathtubs."[2] Among her peers she "kept silent" because she "felt naïve; [and] lacked the perspectives, pedigrees and deep cultural knowledge that my peers brought to the courses."

So what about those like her nurtured in completely antipodean environments to the typical professorial hatchery: are they at a disadvantage in pursuing the professoriate because they were not the progeny of white professors or white-collar professionals?

I saw caste and class issues in action in my first teaching years on the tenure track at Louisiana State University. The mix of students was fascinating and challenging for the newbie teacher: the daughter of an oil company president and the son of a sharecropper sat in the same row. One African American young lady who took several of my courses was the first person in her extended family to attend college. She was a business major, and as she began to consider her career path, she spoke aloud about the possibility of becoming a university educator.

I outlined the steps, as I knew them then, into the professoriate. She heard with some astonishment that, assuming all went well, she would spend two to three years in a master's program, four to five years getting her dissertation, seven on the tenure track, and then another seven to become a "full."[3] She shook her head and said something like, "That's too long to get to *do* anything." I had no effective argument in response.

A few days later she came to my office to ask more about graduate school, and we talked for some time about programs. Then I did not see her until after graduation, when she stopped in to say goodbye. I asked her about possible Ph.D. aspirations. She smiled and said that she had been talked out of it: "My parents—everybody in my family, really—say that I worked hard to get a college degree; why should I waste it going back to school?"

If I were having the conversation today I would have read more of the literature on the "pipeline" of minorities to doctoral programs and tried to contact and enlist African American faculty to mentor her.[4] I would have paid more attention to her *social* filter about a decision to attend graduate school. Research has shown that she had already overcome big hurdles. The graduation rate of students in higher education is affected positively by the level of educational attainment of their parents.[5] "First in family" students have particularly high attrition rates.[6] So I would have made the case that graduate school would build on her successes.[7] I also would have tempered my encouragement with a dose of reality: getting tenure-track jobs in many fields was and is getting tougher and tougher.

Not only, thus, are the doctoral years difficult—and appear even more so to people from family traditions that don't include others who have passed through them—but they are also decisive in affecting *you* and empowering you to affect your own destiny, whatever cards life has dealt you previously. The Ph.D. period is when mindsets and skill sets develop that will either help you advance or will slow or even sabotage your ascent, certainly toward graduation but onward on the tenure track as well. And despite this book being about problems, I know many people who found the brains, moxie, and inventiveness to leap molehills and mountains blocking their path. In graduate school, for example, Benson, the young scholar quoted earlier, "bore down, studied hard and graduated with enough decorations, medals, and awards to set off a metal detector."[8] She is, as of this writing in 2010, an assistant professor at Princeton University.

## All Roads Should Lead to the Dissertation

You are in a doctoral program to propel upward your knowledge base, to mature intellectually, and to advance a field. At no point, however, should you forget that all the assistantships and research projects, the class papers and the studying, the teaching and the socializing must be directed toward conceptualizing, completing, and successfully defending a dissertation. A Ph.D. program that does not end, in a reasonable period, with your getting a doctorate is a waste of your time (and the time and money of other people). The doctoral years are so full of crises, distractions, dead ends, and tangents that if you don't have a streak of ruthlessness and a dash of monomaniacal focus about completing the central project, you won't finish it.

As a simple rule, you should always keep in mind two things:

- How will this help my dissertation?
- How will this hurt my dissertation?

For example, figure out a way for a good part of your class papers and assistantship data to apply to the dissertation. The goal is that by the time you write it up you will have many portions of the document already completed, at least in draft form. The student who traverses four years in a doctoral program and only starts producing content for the dissertation in his fifth year is headed for catastrophe. Staying goal-directed will also help you become a more focused tenure tracker.

Finishing the beast is, by every measure, a great challenge. For example, in my field of mass communications, the time-to-degree is less than five years, while in history it is nearly ten years. Still, that only about 57 percent of the people who start doctoral programs complete them *at all* after a decade is stunning.[9] No wonder that graduate programs are regularly critiqued as being "astonishingly wasteful of their human capital"[10] and even "dystopian" places for the struggling, overworked, underfunded graduate student.[11]

Failure to complete the dissertation is probably the single greatest cause for doctoral delay, decline, and dropout. Some nondissertation reasons offered—ranging from family obligations to health problems—are actually related to the fear, angst, and plain hard work imposed by the demands of the überdocument.

It's not that there aren't lots of how-to resources on dissertation writing. Do a Web search, or read books and articles on the subject, and you'll find thousands of blog posts, memoirs, treatises, and research pieces on dissertation completion, strategies, and tactics.[12] In keeping with the theme of this book, my advice is focused on the people, politics, and personal issues of writing a dissertation, seeing it accepted by a committee, and earning a doctoral degree.

## Don't Write a Dead-Ender . . . But Know Your Ends

The dissertation, no question, will be an immense amount of work, whether you are studying the poems of Pindar or the breeding habits of roseate speckled terns. Nevertheless, doctoral students can waste their dissertations, finishing them but producing documents with no value at all beyond meeting the minimum demand for graduation. The career utility of the document, however, lies in the direction you hope your career will take. Field-specific expectations vary, but here are some general observations.

**A research career demands a research dissertation.** Many times I have met young assistant professors who have just gotten very good tenure-track jobs at high-research universities; they are bright, hardworking, motivated, ambitious, well versed in research methods, and burgeoning experts in their subfield of specialization. Then they tell me, in effect, "I wrote the dissertation just to finish it. I can maybe squeeze a journal article out of it, but to tell you the truth I'm so burned out on the topic that I really don't want to go back there for a while."

Over the last decade, in meeting some authors of dead-end dissertations, I noted how many of them were struggling for tenure as assistant professors. Tragically, these stunted young scholars believe such productivity impoverishment to be a natural state of affairs. No one has explained to them that a dissertation must contribute to earning tenure for its author.

Alarming, thus, are dissertations that may be classified as *dead-enders*. These sad documents almost always share common characteristics:

- *They are short, single-note, or single-point analyses.* Some dissertations are basically one study, usually an experiment or a survey, of one population asking essentially one set of questions with outcomes easily summed up in a few sentences.
- *They are repetitions of previous works.* Judging from their references, cites, and quotes, they are a minor variation on a narrow field of study.
- *They are poorly written.* They are painful reads, probably owing to a general sense of being rushed and insufficiently thought through or fleshed out.

The culprit behind such crimes against scholarship and career advancement is likely not an incompetent Ph.D. candidate or lazy advisers but rather two other human factors that undermine our system of doctoral education.

The first is the haste—even after years of effort!—to finish a dissertation that arises from funding structures and the personal and professional pressures placed on Ph.D. students. Every adviser-professor has heard a doctoral candidate insist, "I have to finish by August 1, or I can't take the job I've been offered" or "I need to defend by the end of the semester because that's when my funding runs out." For we (theoretically) would-be gatekeepers of academic excellence, this is a perennial conundrum. Do we surrender to expediency or defend standards of quality? We faculty assert that we grade by content and not by biography, but we are just as human as our advisees, and find that sometimes sympathy encourages mediocrity.

The second source of a dead-ender is an adviser who has, for whatever reason, decided to use a student's dissertation as an extension of his own work, without regard to whether the text will serve the building of the student's scholarship skills and career portfolio. I will be expanding on signs of this menace.

A dissertation, then, is not something you "just finish." It should, of course, advance our understanding of your topic. But it should also help you in your career, especially if you will go on to a tenure-track or post-doc job with a strong research expectation. It should be a wellspring, a goody bag, a key helper in achieving tenure. As a very wise dean once told me during my master's years, in our field (mass communication) a dissertation should be the source of at least six journal articles and/or one book. A doctoral student should write a dissertation with publications in mind. A career-wise committee and a shrewd adviser will help you in this process. In fact, if you find your adviser and committee pushing you toward a dissertation that serves no purpose except to get you out the door, it's time for a new adviser and a new committee.

In addition, although the exigencies of publication in individual fields are beyond the focus of this book, the publishing expectations for doctoral students have increased in the last generation. When I got my Ph.D., a single published paper would have distinguished a doctoral student as a high achiever. Now, the most recent hire (in 2010) I made as director of a school was ABD with four publications and two more on the way. Simply put, in most fields, if you don't "think publish" or "show publish" you will be much more likely to be unemployed—at least if you hope to work at a research university.

In practice, writing the dissertation with future publication in mind means two things: writing to publish (eventually), and writing to build a network of contacts.

Toward publishing, the writing style, substance, and structure should not be radically different from the publication forms of your field. Ideally, each post–"lit review" chapter might fit well as an article for submission to a conference; perhaps the entire dissertation might morph into a monograph. Compromises are inevitable, but if you find yourself, in the first years of the tenure track, flailing around starting up new research projects, you are in trouble. In fact, the senior faculty will think there is something wrong with you if your dissertation begets nothing but a line in your curriculum vitae (CV).

**The teaching or modest research dissertation is another matter.** All the above applies if your plan is to try to get a job at a university with moderate or high research expectations. But what if you don't? As of this writing in spring 2010, some disciplines are reeling with yet another crisis of hiring. In history, the languages, and economics, the number of positions open is dropping sharply while more and more Ph.D. students graduate, looking for their first position. The backlog of unemployed doctorate-holders grows and grows. No surprise that increasingly schools are accepting the idea of a "teaching dissertation." As one chair of a history department put it, "There are many people who just want to teach and are happy to get a job. They'll end up somewhere where the dissertation's sole purpose is a line item on a CV." Such tenure trackers don't need to write a publication-intended dissertation.

A case in point is history, a discipline for which a research dissertation is almost always defined as a publishable book—that is, a monograph that will be converted for publication by a reputable university press and will garner laudatory reviews in academic journals. But one history doctoral student at a midtier program told his adviser, "I don't want this to be a tome." His intention—which he fulfilled—was to get a job at a small liberal arts college, write a few articles, get tenure, teach as much as was expected, and maybe down the road tinker with the manuscript, perhaps over decades, to ultimately turn it into a book. He did not, nor do many doctoral students, have the "yearn to burn"— the expectation that the only possible career was one that demanded a high research bar.

Many doctoral programs will accommodate you if you do not see yourself as a lifelong researcher. That's the personal context in three Ps. The people and politics wild card is that, even in lower-tier doctoral programs, there are professors who worship the creed that *all* dissertations should be heavy research dissertations. They may try to talk you into the research track, and maybe they will convince you. But you need to be fully aware of the expectations of either direction of your career. One sociology doctoral student at a lower-tier program described an adviser who came off like a frustrated Texas football dad who'd sublimated his own hopes and dreams of a pro career into his protégé progeny. "He kept talking about how important it was to produce this big research document as if that was the only thing I could do. But I didn't want that. He wasn't listening." The student found a new adviser.

**The dissertation is a tool for networking.** You should also write the dissertation to build relationships for your future—including the relationships that will help you get a job.[13] Here is a strategy that one business professor, my father, found to be successful for almost half a century for graduate students, mostly MBAs, at an Ivy League institution: if students chose to do a master's project or thesis with him, he would ask them, "What would you like to do after graduation, what company do you want to work for, what industry, what market, doing what?" Then he would direct them to write a thesis that would serve as a tool for attaining those ends. If, for example, a student answered, "I'm fascinated by the steel industry, I love marketing, and my mother is from Ecuador and I'm bilingual," her big project could be a paper on some subject like expanding U.S. steel company markets in Latin America.

Here was the genius in the system: to write her thesis, the student would call up the major steel executives at American and international companies and interview them. (They would respond to being asked for their "expertise.") She would then write up a pertinent report and send it to the contacts with thanks. She found, as did many other students, that establishing relations personally and preemptively—rather than via the more ex post facto and impersonal route of working through the human resources department—led to an open door when the time for the job search came around.

The same method works well in academia at the doctoral level. Don't just quote the (living) luminary scholars in your area by reading their works. Correspond with them; ask for a few minutes of their time and some words of advice at conferences; offer your help in their own research. These are the people who one day may hire you, or script job reference letters for you, or even write your outside evaluation letters for tenure. Why not let them get to know your face, name, and interests now? Again, good human relations are not in opposition to advancing your knowledge.

## Stay Healthy in Mind and Body

Completing graduate school is a physical and mental effort, so to advocate that you should find some kind of regular physical exercise and stick to it is not outside our task here. The mental health benefits of running, biking, swimming, and long walks are documented. Furthermore, the brain is assisted by a good diet as much as is the cardiovascular system. Pizza and caffeine may have gotten you through final exams as a sophomore, but half a decade of daily labor on a dissertation will be sustained only by something more substantial. Yes, you will redeye through many nights without sleep; yes, you will skip meals or load up on too much Mountain Dew; but don't sacrifice your bodily health. It is a key helper to getting along and successfully getting out of a doctoral program and sustaining you on the tenure track.

There are, in addition, distractions that actually help one concentrate on a central project. Many great people have found that their day job is enhanced if they find other activities, in parallel, to which they can devote their minds and time, such as painting or some other creative art.[14] Some superior academics play musical instruments or cast clay pots. It does not matter what your hobby (a rather inadequate word) is as long as it rejuvenates and refreshes you so that you can return to the big kahuna of your dissertation with a clear mind.

Finally, there is a case, both philosophical and scientific, for not thinking that you should always be thinking about the document alone. Let's call it Zen and the Art of the Dissertation.[15] Writing a dissertation involves a lot of grinding work, but for many people, perhaps most, the intellectual breakthroughs that helped advance the project came tacitly: they just came, they could not be forced. Developing some way to clear the mind through yoga, prayer, biofeedback, visualization training, t'ai chi, or just playing Frisbee is useful.

I myself did something that I would not recommend for everyone but which certainly helped me finish my degree: I embarked on a completely unrelated substantial project. My dissertation was a huge content analysis that involved thousands of images in magazines, lots of archival sifting, and much background reading—and writing, writing, and more writing. About six months into it, I was bored out of my mind. Although I still found the topic intriguing, the process was painful, and worse, I found many blocks to intellectual creativity. I did not like what I was writing. I knew it wasn't good. So I decided to start a major new research project with a wholly different kind of method and theory. I called my local police department and asked if I could ride along with officers and take pictures for a visual ethnography of police. I even joined the department as a reserve officer.

Incredibly, my great diversionary gambit succeeded because the new project itself was so rewarding. Two to three nights a week I rode along with the cops, taking notes and pictures. During the day I worked on "the beast." The latter labor started to go well. Somehow the adrenaline, activity, and strong differences in the night research helped me focus on the day research.

## Communicate Maturity and Responsibility

Impression management, or what sociologist Erving Goffman called the "presentation of self," is vital in any business. How others in academe, especially deans, and P&T committee members, and peers in your field—not to mention students, staff, and others—appraise you is critical to your career success. As a graduate student, you are in a strange, liminal (between two worlds) situation: you are both a student and someone expected to assume many of the behaviors and duties of faculty members, such as teaching and research. But one day people will hire you (even as a post-doc) not because they want a great student but because they want a great colleague. Two character traits stand out as good for you and good for your image: maturity and responsibility.

Graduate school is the best place to learn how to convince people you possess those qualities. Don't underestimate how important maturity and responsibility are to P&T. We live in an age in which childish behavior by adults, from billionaires to politicians to professional athletes to reality show contestants, is common. Maybe that's not a problem if you play basketball or are a rock star or plan to make your living eating bugs on television. But one place where acting like a petulant child will lose you much and gain you nothing is definitely graduate school and the tenure track. Impress your supervisors, advisers, and fellow students by keeping cool, calm, and collected, showing due diligence, and not being a perpetual whiner.

For example, during the writing of this book, when I was at another university, one of our faculty members died suddenly. She was teaching a basic writing course for which about three weeks were left in the term. Her graduate teaching assistant, whom I will call Mr. Loras, was still a first-year master's student. He immediately helped us collect the professor's mail, notifying sometimes distraught students, retrieving grade books, and then, without extra payment, volunteering to teach the remaining classes. He notably took on the new labors efficiently and without complaint. The undergraduate students, upset by the tragic event, responded well to his maturity and responsibility.

When he was later applying to doctoral programs, I wrote the following in his reference letter:

> Mr. Loras stepped in and worked hard to complete the professor's section for the year, not only teaching but pulling together the late instructor's materials and making sure that the students were given all the necessary tests and grades. Mr. Loras performed such "above and beyond" service without complaint and with cool professionalism. Several undergraduates expressed their appreciation for what he did for them as well as for the school.

The outcome? He was accepted with full funding to four major doctoral programs in our field and chose the one he felt was best for his course of study. His conduct after the tragedy was only one of many reasons that graduate programs were attracted to him, but I do feel that his virtue was rewarded. As one of the faculty in a program that made him an offer told me, "The kind of conscientiousness you talked about in your letter really stood out. We need people like that as professors."

## Adapting to Graduate School Culture

Although a doctoral student's primary goal is to finish a dissertation, the many years in a program are not only about reading, experimenting, and writing. When assessing Ph.D. success, research suggests that two concepts are of use and at play in your life. The first is *social integration*—that is, how much you find yourself fitting into the social world of the school.[16] Then there is *academic integration*, the fit into the institution's culture of learning. Ten variables seem to influence the latter, with some being more important than others to individuals, groups, or overall:[17]

- quality of advising
- feelings of fitting into classroom culture
- interactions with faculty and other students
- kinds and frequency of assistantships
- level of funding support
- level of working with faculty or other students on research
- mentoring systems and individual mentoring relationships
- participation in research publishing
- perceptions of classroom climate
- teaching load

A major factor affecting integration is who you are. It is fine to advise graduate students to get together with peers, but you need to find peers who help and inspire you, not drag you down. (I will talk more about this issue later because it applies to tenure-track peers as well.) Consider this observation made by a researcher looking at, in part, the effect of the race of graduate students on their selection of friends in their programs:

> The most consistent pattern in peer interactions existed among the
> Black participants, male and female, graduates and currently enrolled

students. Blacks often connected with other Black students whenever possible. When asked why she did not interact as much with her White peers, one woman stated, "To be honest, I think it was the sheer cultural differences. I was from a southern, African-American culture and that whole scene, I came to a northern culture that consisted of, primarily, at least in my department, [mid]westerners who were White. And, I think that neither of us was very comfortable interacting with each other."[18]

Certainly, many groups, from gays to Asian Americans, find support in kin-peers. On the other hand, there is also a case for building networks and finding key allies and mentors *across* the divides of class, culture, race, ethnicity, and sexual preference. Some research has shown, for example, that faculty tend to select assistants who are most like them in several attributes, including ethnicity—decisions that can leave out in the cold grad students who come from minorities underrepresented among faculty ranks.[19]

One female Muslim graduate student addressed this point. She wore a head scarf and, in accordance with her tradition, did not shake hands with men. From a few of her peers and professors in her graduate program she felt prejudice. But from most she sensed uncertainty about how to interact with her and a reluctance to get any closer as friend or mentor. She could likely have connected with other Muslim women, but there were none in her program. So she went to extra lengths to reach out—to employ Edward T. Hall's admonition to "meet them half way"—making friends among fellow students and finding professors who acted as good mentors/advisers. She made the best of an imperfect situation. The outcomes of such actions are worth the exertion. While faculty should certainly do their best to engage you, many need signals that you welcome the effort.

## Family and Friends: Encouragers and Inhibitors

I mentioned earlier a young African American woman whom I had failed to encourage sufficiently to pursue graduate school. Her decision was probably due in part to kin-pressure: Her non-college-educated family saw no point in her going past the B.A. degree.[20] Those of us who are not clinical psychologists or psychiatrists with a focus on family therapy are not fully qualified to comment on the interrelations of family dynamics and careers, but, as said, the research generally supports the notion that the fewer educational attainments of one's parents, the less likely one is to succeed in advancing in higher education. Human beings, however, are not walking stereotypes. We all have the power either to overcome or to impair our predoctoral, pre-tenure-track legacies.

For example, a doctoral student in the second year of her program in the physical sciences is newly married and is in a field where there are reasonable paying opportunities for someone with a degree at the master's level. No one in her family has gone beyond an undergraduate degree, and her husband is a business professional. She is facing the dilemma of many academics in that, when she goes to school—to study, to conduct research, to engage faculty and her cohort—she is entering into a world very different from that of her extra-academic friends and family.

They are not cheerleading for her to fail or actively sabotaging; they just don't understand the true requirements of her doctoral studies. Typically, for instance, the husband cannot comprehend why his labors end at 5 o'clock but hers do not. Why does she need to stay late at the library or meet with a study group? Why does she need to get up in the middle of the night to write? Why can't she plan her vacations as formally as he does his? Mother, father, and extended relatives find it strange that in her early thirties she has chosen to become a "student" for four or more years just to get the chance to become a "post-doc" and then an "assistant." And why can't she pinpoint, within a decade, her date of graduation?

In another case, a master's student has applied to several doctoral programs. He is admitted to one that is within driving distance of his family, but he also is admitted to other programs that are across the country. The family is puzzled why it isn't a natural choice to stay close to home. He cannot articulate his feeling to them that without loved ones in proximity he would be able to get more work done. Nor is the family able to gauge the substantive differences in quality or focus or faculty among doctoral programs with the same title.

A solution for such impasses is to spend some time talking to your family about academia itself. No need for a PowerPoint presentation at the next Thanksgiving gathering; rather, explain to them exactly what you think will be required of you in the four or more years devoted to completing a doctoral program. Don't frame this as "what you need to do for me"—you yourself will probably have to make compromises. It is unreasonable, for example, to tell parents, "I won't be home for Christmas anymore because I'll be busy studying." Instead, describe how this business is not like a lot of others with which they are probably more familiar.

A key persuasive element is not to make a doctoral education and the tenure track sound like a cross to bear; family will only question even more the wisdom of your decision. But stress how critical this enterprise is to you. Use elements from your application's personal essay here, explaining how the academic life is a promise to fulfill certain needs within you. In short, try to get your family to understand, if not share, your passion and your drive. Emphasize the delayed but eventual rewards that come with success in our business: job security, a decent income that does not fluctuate wildly with changes in the economy, autonomy of time, summers to spend with family, the respect of peers in the community.

## Getting Along with Faculty

Smooth relations with fellow students in a doctoral program are of great benefit. But research on the subject[21] and innumerable anecdotes testify that the most significant human relationships in graduate school are with faculty. For the good, they will help propel your career to glory; for the ill, they can ruin your dreams and land you in therapy.

To ground your faculty relations on a sober, nondramatic level, start out by repeating the following as often as you can: *It's not all about me!* Graduate students can get flustered because of what they perceive as bad treatment by a professor; other times they get excited at praise from a faculty member. In both cases, the eventual outcome might not be, respectively, dejection or elation but rather relief and disappointment because (a) the first faculty member was not hostile but was instead indifferent to your fate, or (b) the second's enthusiasm was fleeting, like the beam of the lighthouse, momentarily focused and then pointed somewhere else.

In illustration, here's a story about a doctoral candidate confronting what he thought would be a terrible "human relations" poser. He had asked Professor Noire to chair his committee. But then he changed his mind about what topic he wanted to focus on, and it was clear that Professor Blanche was actually the better choice for that topic. So he was conflicted and stressed: how could he tell the first one that he was, in effect, firing her for someone else? Would he hurt her feelings? Would she get mad? Would she retaliate somehow?

It was a truly trepidatious moment when the student stopped by Noire's office and haltingly delivered the bad news. Surprisingly, she took it well, wishing the student the best on the new direction in research. No drama, no problem—big surprise. Another professor later explained the rationale of his colleague thus:

> Look, we like you, but we like our own work and time and family better, so when you come to us and say, I am letting you off the hook for hundreds of hours of reading, counseling, meetings, memos, exams, and all the work that comes with being a dissertation adviser, our inner response is "Whoopee!"

Ah, insight! In other words, do not fret and thrill with every comment from your faculty advisers. You are on a long road. You cannot afford to be anxious or exhilarated at every bump and turn.

That said, not all faculty will play equally weighty roles in your Ph.D. life. Ten years after your defense, you won't remember the names of some professors in your doctoral program; others will remain intimate friends. In larger programs with lots of subfields, you may meet Professor Dondarrion only at school functions, take one required class from Professor Mormont, but spend part of every day of the school year in a lab with Professor Tully. The last pairing is the crucial one. All the research agrees that *the single most important human relationship you have with faculty is with your mentors and dissertation adviser.* To that we may add another classification of faculty: your supervisor in research or teaching assistantships. Of course, the mentor/adviser/supervisor may all be the same person.

## The Most Key Relationship: Mentor and Protégé

Ever since I was in graduate school, I have quizzed or formally surveyed doctoral students, mostly in the social sciences and humanities, about their ideal academic adviser. High on their wish list:

- Someone who is respected within the field and has contacts who can help with publications and jobs.
- Someone who is knowledgeable about the university and its politics and policies.
- Someone who takes the time to help with studies and career.
- Someone who is not exploitative.
- Someone who is not a disinterested observer but who cares and is supportive, like a coach cheering you on.

I once shared that list with a senior colleague who has a reputation as a great mentor, and he chuckled at its optimistic comprehensiveness and walk-on-water expectation.

But that doesn't mean Ph.D. students should stop hoping to discover "Dr. Right"; in fact, the profile is similar to how junior faculty members on the tenure track would describe their ideal career mentor. What is not widely understood is that the other side of the relationship—how to be a good protégé—has its own strategies, techniques, and responsibilities. Perhaps getting advice seems a more clear-cut task than giving it. But at a time when budding academics seem busier and pulled in more directions than ever, it is all the more important to understand how to learn from a mentor.

Some veteran professors also note a strong cultural gap in temperament and outlook between themselves and new faculty members. Typically this is posited as Boomers versus Gen X versus Gen Y, an issue faced in all forms of professional enterprise, not just academia.[22] Whatever the reason, failing to seek, find, and keep a productive relationship with a mentor during the tenure-track years and beyond is a serious mistake.

As Ph.D. students or faculty, we can always use help—good help—and we need to know how to get it and keep it coming. Moreover, the whole system of academia depends on faculty having capable assistants with whom to work. So how do both sides help each other? How do you become and stay a good protégé?

A bedrock quality of a valued and valuable protégé is being able to accept imperfection in mentors. You can get useful counsel from people who may not possess all, or even most, of the attributes of the perfect mentor or the perfect person. A doctoral student once lamented that a senior professor in her department, while offering astute advice about research methods, was a cold fish when it came to personal encouragement. My response: Listen carefully to what he says about content analysis but find somebody else to be your confidant.

Alternately, there was a Grand Old Man who was a true father confessor to his doctoral students, the perfect sounding board with whom they could share their worries and leave feeling buoyed and respected. The problem was that he was too positive in his critiques of research: all the presentations he witnessed were "wonderful!" All the papers he read were "terrific!" Worse, he dispensed misguided advice about "only applying for jobs to peer programs" because "you are the best and the best will hire you." His students indeed felt good about themselves, until the rejections started rolling in, for papers and then for jobs, and they began to catch on that the rest of the academic world did not view them through the same rosy glow as did their mentor. One of his advisees, years later, referred to herself as a "recovering Golden Child" because it had taken her quite some time to realize that sobriety of assessment was preferable to effusive but blind praise.

That an individual faculty member may not be all wrong or right on every subject is something that most graduate students discover after a while, but even so, discerning their actual from their famed or titular levels of expertise is crucial. A doctoral student described an exhilarating conversation with a senior faculty member who urged him to write his dissertation on a particular topic. Only years later did the student learn that that subarea of study was considered antiquarian and passé by the majority of researchers in the discipline. It was a significant problem for his job search that his specialization was something few people were interested in anymore. He realized that, however well meaning his adviser had been, the old man was clueless about the modern trends in the field, or perhaps was unwilling to admit that his own work was considered stale and irrelevant.

The ideal adviser, thus, may be a composite of various imperfect humans. Understanding that fact allows you to better estimate what a mentor can and can't do for you. I recall telling a master's student, many years ago, that I would be happy to write him a letter of recommendation to doctoral programs in which I had friends on the faculty, but I could not guarantee his admission. The look of doubt on his face prompted me to repeat the caveat. When I asked him why he was viewing me with skepticism, he stated that his parents and close acquaintances had always gotten him the jobs he sought and he assumed academe worked the same way.

The opposite problem arises when the protégé is too passive about asking for help. One of my graduate students was turned down for a job at an institution where I knew the dean and several faculty well; the student had never asked me to write a letter or make a phone call on her behalf. Her rationale was, "I didn't want to bother you." Her reticence in this instance, I realized, was my fault: I had made the mistake of mentioning in class that, because I was a faculty member in my middle years of academic life, writing letters of recommendation for present and former students had become a "part-time job." I had not meant to imply that I didn't want to write such letters. My student, however, came from a country where professors hold a sacerdotal status and so took my jest as a brush-off.

Establishing clear communications, sometimes across the borders of age and culture, is thus a key to clarifying what can be asked of mentor and protégé. That's the ideal, but it is hard to achieve it if either party doesn't ask for help.

The good protégé also appreciates the borders of the relationship with a mentor. You want to be on pleasant terms, of course, but there is such a thing as overfraternization, not only regarding the obvious minefield of romantic liaisons but also the impositions that too much friendliness can bring to both parties. A minor example is the issue of time: one junior faculty member became such good friends with her adviser that every meeting they had to talk ostensibly about research was taken up, in part, by family news and gossip. They were both busy people, so they ultimately agreed to cover all personal conversation in a maximum of five minutes during future meetings. When protégé and mentor are too close, their differential status can muddle things. A friend might ask you to house-sit or do other favors, but is it appropriate for mentors to make such requests of their advisees? More infamous (and alarming) are the advisers who insist on being listed as coauthors on published studies even when their contributions are minimal. But the risk of imposition cuts both ways. A professor recounted that a young scholar at a different university had asked for his help on a project and was so satisfied with the result that requests for further assistance started to arrive daily. A good protégé does not make too many demands on an adviser.

Next, learn to accept criticism gracefully. We all know a Fragile Freddie who breaks down at any hint of negativity, discards student evaluations without reading them, and never looks at article reviews. A useful mentor is one who is willing to give us bad news and a wise protégé wants to hear it. Both parties must be sensitive to the degree of independence the protégé wants (and needs) from the mentor. Students who can't seem to navigate their research, teaching, and service obligations without the guiding mind and hand of their doctoral mentor will fatally carry that dependency on to the tenure track. They seem to produce no original research; all their work is either co-authored with the mentor or apes his or her style.

Accept also that the protégé-mentor bond may simply fade away. Say your mentor loses interest in a certain research area, becomes busy with other colleagues, or goes through a period of personal distraction. Politeness and kindness are called for, but there is no written contract that demands that you return to the same well for advice forever. A fruitful, long-lasting mentor–protégé relationship is one of the great joys of an academic career. But like any meeting of minds, it needs to be worked at, tended carefully, and evaluated for its boundaries as well as appreciated for its opportunities.

Further, graduate students (and assistant professors) must avoid faculty squabbles. But sometimes when you select an adviser, you are inadvertently picking a fight. Take this scenario: a young scholar interviews for a tenure-track job and, having done his homework, tells the hiring committee that he looks forward to working with Professor Capulet. Well, he is hired, and from day one Professor Montague treats him coolly. It turns out that the pair have been feuding for years, and now the tenure tracker is marked as a partisan. He will have to work at finding the balance between collaborating in research with one faculty member but also convincing the other that he is not a political enemy. Alternately, you may find it wise to simply avoid working with one professor or another because he has a reputation of drawing in students or junior faculty to his political struggles.

Good senior advisers will appreciate that graduate students and junior faculty members should stay out of the way when the elephants snort and rumble. Even if they are embroiled in a scrap, the best advisers won't drag you into it and will shelter you from it.

A final sign that your mentors may be qualified for the post is that they recognize and disclose their own strengths and limitations. For example, Professor Adams helps you design a syllabus for your new course in an area in which she has taught for years. You appreciate the assistance, noting how she pointed out problems and issues that you would never have thought of. You follow up and ask her advice on grading term papers, and she says, "You know, I've always struggled with that. You might ask Professor Jefferson. He is a master of the essay question." Well, you have now shined the lantern on at least one honest mentor. You can be reasonably sure that in the future, when Dr. Adams feels her advice is worth offering, you can bank on it.

So the perfect mentor is uncommon. Still, academe is overflowing with many honorable and wise men and women who give up their time and energy to help up-and-coming colleagues.

Here is a contrarian thought, however. Having a great mentor or mentors is almost always a positive, but in any considerations of the three Ps of career advancement in academia, the possible negatives must be weighed as well. These may be less apparent during the doctoral years but more so when you go on the job market or become an assistant professor. Both of these caveats might be classified as "mentor blowback."

**Me and my shadow.** Great men and women—in war, politics, or academia—cast umbras that may make their protégés glow or that may obscure their individuality. A senior geologist once lamented that, for the first twenty years of his career, he was still mostly known as "a student of the famous Dr. Luster." The superstar had been his doctoral adviser; they had copublished heavily, all to the "student's" benefit. The protégé gained from the association; it helped him get his first job. But over the years he had begun to worry that he was not establishing a truly individual track of research, and indeed a name. He ended up branching off into a new area of study, not just because of its intellectual interest but because he "didn't want to retire as a footnote to someone else's career."

There is no perfect way to balance the detriment of losing your individuality with the benefit of being helped by a major figure in your discipline. But anyone in a doctoral program and on the tenure track, and certainly in the years beyond as an associate professor, should think about how to establish an independent profile. It should not deny those who have helped us and tutored us but should cast us in our own light for our own achievements.

**Famous or infamous?** I have no proof that the green-eyed monster rampages more viciously in academia than in, say, the music industry or waste management. But envy is a part of our business, and a simple rule is, the greater the heights you reach, the more likely there will be other people who wouldn't mind seeing you reveal feet of clay. And, let's face it, it is difficult to rise to the top without making some enemies, for whatever reason.

The catch is that with fame and repute comes power, and people may not be willing to snipe at the powerful or attempt some bureaucratic measure against them. The graduate student, post-doc, and assistant professor protégés of the Great Woman, on the other hand, are more vulnerable targets. As discussed in the chapter on job searching, it is possible that a letter of reference from the great and well-praised but also widely disliked Dr. Luster will provoke some silent antagonist of his on the search committee to wreak revenge by vetoing your candidacy.

## Improving Graduate Assistantships

Hopefully, as part of your doctoral experience you received a research or teaching appointment: the assistantship. The financial reward for such jobs is often low, at least relative to that of an outside job, so much so that graduate research assistants (GRAs) and graduate teaching assistants (GTAs) may need to supplement their income with other employment.[23]

All of my advice is predicated on two facts. First, your assistantship is a real job, and you must treat it seriously. Second, whatever good or bad comes from the assistantship, it will prepare you for similar duties and human relations issues in the tenure-track years to come.

For some, the assistantship experience can truly be inspiring. A student in cinema studies was lucky enough to become a teaching assistant for an exceptional film scholar. Within a year she was promoted to graduate teaching associate, which meant she had three regular GTAs helping her help the professor in his large lecture classes. She even got to substitute for the professor in giving lectures when he was away. It was a job that allowed her to appreciate firsthand some aspects of being a higher educator—and love it.

At the other end of the spectrum was a GRA assigned to an assistant professor in a humanities department. His boss was a young star in a subfield that interested him as a dissertation topic, and he asked her to be his adviser. But now it's his fourth year in the program, and he is getting no guidance on his dissertation; his supervisor does not seem even to be reading the chapters he sends her. The assistantship is foundering as well. The assistant professor has not been able to finish the book she is writing and next year she will go up for tenure. The student senses she is in a panic about her career, and he feels the same way about his own situation.

There are indeed many varieties of assistantships, as well as many outcomes. So how does one make the most of graduate assistantship time and duties?

First and foremost, understand that any anxieties you may feel are normal, but they are not insurmountable. Most faculty who supervise

GTAs and GRAs genuinely hope to make the experience a mutually beneficial one. Also, you are protected by (and should be held accountable to) the rules and laws of your institution and the state. But, in a situation that foreshadows the uncertainty of the tenure-track years, you are, after all, pretty low on the food chain of academia. The multitudes of despairing posts on the *Chronicle of Higher Education* forums and graduate student blogs and wikis testify that assistantships, although sometimes enriching, can be Dantesque nightmares.

There are constructive steps you can take to ward off trouble even before your assistantship starts, to avoid problems during the assistantship, and to escape from truly hellish situations.

Begin with a simple precept, held by as varying advocates as the people of Bali, the Roman emperor Marcus Aurelius, and every truly accomplished academic: "Whatsoever thy hand findeth to do, do it with thy might" (Eccles. 9:10). In other words: *If you commit to doing something, do it as well as you can.*

So, for example, you may be a high-flyer doctoral student, feeling sure of your bright future as a theorist. But to survive financially you take a teaching assistantship that consists primarily of grading undergraduate papers and handing out class materials. You are not intellectually challenged at all. Well, that's too bad. In a perfect world you would be advancing theory with sage-like mentors for a huge stipend. In the real world, you have an ethical and practical choice before you. Do you (a) slough off the work, doing the least you can, the least well you can get away with? or (b) do the work as well as you can and provide good service to the school, the students, and your supervisor?

The correct answer is *b*. Throughout your career you will be obliged to devote time to duties that you (and others) may perceive to be menial. Better to find ways to complete them efficiently and comprehensively from the outset. In addition, keep in mind that you are doing a job for which someone—the taxpayers, a funding agency, or the professor herself—is *paying*. You owe each of them, and the students, a decent return. By your competent efforts, you will nurture those character traits that I argued earlier are among the most vital for a starter faculty member both to have and to be recognized as having: *responsibility* and *maturity*. When a hiring committee is perusing letters of recommendation, those two words pop out as exemplary. Why not use GRA and GTA experiences to showcase your readiness for the tenure track and beyond?

Again, as well, the virtuous can also be practical. Be the kind of assistant you will want to supervise yourself some day. Appreciate that, for instance, grading those papers is great training.

Even before a graduate assistantship begins you can initiate a process of trying to make it, if not edifying, at least disaster-free. You should meet your prospective boss and carefully review your expected duties and outcomes. Now is the time to ask about deadlines and the scope and feasibility of the projects or work. Be candid about your skill sets and ask for more instruction where you think you need it.

In these early meetings you should also request, and perhaps even design yourself, a system of reporting your progress toward the project goals. Records of accomplishment must always be in print and dated: something as simple as an e-mail noting, "Dr. Bolton: I'd like to list the work I have completed for the last week."

Such a system will serve you as well as the work itself in several ways. It keeps you (and the supervisor) focused on what has been done and what is coming next. It provides regular feedback that can help improve the work and your performance. It establishes a record that you can cite if any problems occur in the future—such as, in a worst case, when your supervisor decides (retroactively) that he is dissatisfied with your efforts.

Next, make sure you have gotten all the preparation you need and beyond, whether it is with SPSS or Microsoft Outlook or the Human Subjects Committee certification. Try to frontload formal training, such as in classes on software, as early as possible because your time will only get more constricted as the semester flies by. Above all, read your institutional policies that govern assistantships.

Now raise the question of the anticipated outcomes for you and your work. You could ask for "primer" sessions during the term where your supervisor explains why and how she is managing and teaching the course the way she is. In the case of research assistantships, if you see opportunities for providing data for your own studies, specify early what both you and your supervisor expect them to be. Project any publishing goals, and the authorship bylines, that might result from the research. Again, all such plans should end up in writing.

As is clear, the grad assistantship is work but it also constitutes a human relationship. Any collaboration between people has the potential for trouble due to conflicting personalities, work styles, and goals. Some supervisor–graduate assistant mismatches are the stuff of stereotype, such as the egomaniacal senior professor who exploits the naïve and nervous assistant. But the dialectic of control can swing the other way: uncertain, harried young assistant professors can be bullied by assertive, overly confident GRAs or GTAs.

No matter how much planning and forethought you engage in, unforeseen problems—the sick relative or the sudden onslaught of assignments in another course—may always surface. Not all faculty have the same attitude toward this issue, but in general most of us would prefer both candor and a timely heads-up. We are willing to change the schedule, but we want to know why the work will be done late, when it will be made up, and that the quality will not suffer.

Faculty patience will also evaporate when, week after week, new troubles erupt. Even the kindliest supervisor might say: "Look, you have too many things going on in your life to do this job." A graduate assistantship is not an entitlement program. You have institutional, legal, and human rights, but preparation, communication, and honesty will go a long way toward preventing troubles before they start.

How you and the supervisor treat each other in public is also pertinent. We are currently witnessing the collapse of deference and the rise of egalitarianism in society, but graduate assistants should know their role, especially when interacting with the supervisor in the presence of undergraduates. Certainly, nobody wants to take a class from a dictator. But, on the other hand, students look to professors for structure, order, and authority. Teaching assistants should contribute to this climate by being supportive of the instructor. Remember that one day you will (you hope) be in the same position and will likewise not appreciate a smart-aleck or undermining GTA.

Sometimes undergraduate students will bring classroom problems to you, the graduate assistant, because you are younger, more accessible, or less intimidating than the professor. They may lament that the work is too hard or the grading is unfair. You may be tempted to score popularity points and commiserate with them. Don't. In many cases you may not be experienced enough to know whether a student complaint is warranted. Nor does it help the undergrads if they get mixed messages about, say, grading criteria. Better to try to positively and constructively resolve the difficulty in conjunction with your supervisor.

The other side of the coin is when you feel that the professor is not supporting *you*. Sometimes an insecure assistant professor uses the GTA as a "straight man" for or as the butt of jokes to curry favor with students. Or a boorish senior professor thinks GTA means "flunky to humiliate." In such situations, you have few choices. You can strike back in class in front of the undergraduates, but that nuclear option will only gain you a few moments' fun. You can make a formal complaint, especially if you think that the "joking" has become abusive. You can grin and bear it and try to switch assistantships thereafter. Or you can try to talk out the problem with the professor.

The degree, extent, and quality of your supervision also matter. You might worry about getting a micromanager boss who stands over your shoulder telling you what to do all of the time. If you are dealing with explosive chemicals or undergraduates, that may not be such a bad thing. Different people have different comfort levels. You may have to put up with an overbearing boss and keep smiling.

The flip side is feedback deficit: when you don't feel you are getting enough instruction about what the professor wants you to do. Worse, you may not find out about trouble until it is too late to address or correct it. There are many reasons why professors undersupervise. They get busy and distracted; they may not really know themselves what they want; they seek to avoid conflict; or they may just be inept managers. Dealing with an uncertain, shy, or absent boss can be more tricky than dealing with a hands-on one: sometimes you just have to let things slide, other times you may have to speak up, requesting more direction. If you really feel there is a problem, document it, perhaps writing a note to yourself by e-mail (which dates your issue). Approaching another faculty member or the administration should be left to complaints about actual harassment (as will be discussed), not "my supervisor does not give me enough instructions."

Being undersupervised may also be an opportunity for you to shine. After all, one of the great attractions of our business is that we, as faculty, are much less overseen than most other workers. Professors may have dozens of graduate assistants in a career. Ratings of whether they are poor or excellent in the work may depend on the type of assignment they have. When tedious, rote work needs to be done—content analysis coding, collection of archival files—the GRA need not be creative, just accurate and deliberate. Other times, when research is more open-ended, like looking for literature on a new topic, entrepreneurial creativity can be welcome. Being a professor, as well as a grad student, requires both qualities, and an assistantship is a good place to try to improve or develop each within yourself.

Even if the graduate assistantship road is rocky, it can be a learning moment that contributes to your later full-time academic career. When I was working toward my doctorate, I was a GTA in a general survey course. Just before final exams, I substituted for the professor in a review session for the undergraduates. Unfortunately, I did not prepare for the meeting, thinking I could wing it. Several times, the students stumped me with pretty basic (but consequential) questions about course themes and facts. Standing up there on the podium, with forty undergrads staring at me thinking either (a) this guy is an idiot or (b) this guy really blew off his job, I felt mortified and vowed never again to enter a classroom unprepared. Whenever I feel overworked and am tempted to forgo class preparation, the memory of my early tribulation keeps me on target.

It was a bad experience but a good lesson, which can sum up being a graduate assistant sometimes. Yes, there are true worst-case scenarios, such as sexual harassment or professors involving you in fraud. But most often a graduate assistantship, whether focused on research or teaching, is a necessary primer on the greater adventure of becoming a professor.

# The Academic Job Search

Job hunting, whether you are already on the P&T track or not, is one of the murkiest activities of academia because so many intangible elements come into play. You fail to get an offer because somebody misunderstood a sentence in your application letter or never bothered to attend your on-campus presentation, or because some senior faculty felt threatened by your precocious achievements. You do get a job because the top three candidates turned the school down, somebody was particularly impressed by your teaching philosophy statement, or the dean perceived you as pliable and not likely to be a troublemaker.

Read wikis, blogs, or online forums about job searching and you will be regaled with many anecdotes of catastrophes, poor treatment, and faux pas. But even then, when everything seems to go wrong, it may simply be a test of those two defining qualities whose importance I stressed earlier: maturity and responsibility. A search committee chair in a language department described "the campus visit from hell" that a young doctoral student suffered when applying to his unit. Her luggage was lost; a fellow passenger on the airplane spilled coffee on the clothes she was wearing; the car of the search committee member who picked her up at the airport got a flat, and he, elderly and frail, had to watch as she changed the tire; a rainstorm drove down attendance at her presentations; there was a glitch in the PowerPoint software that mysteriously inserted weird characters into her slides; and so on. Through it all, the young woman remained poised, indefatigable, and of good cheer. The search committee was duly impressed, feeling that if she could survive and keep cool and professional under those trying circumstances, she would very likely fare well as a teacher and researcher. She got the job.

More often what went wrong—that is, if you did anything wrong at all—may never be revealed to you. Rejection generally arrives via a generic form letter (paper or e-mail) that employs the ritualistic, "We had an unusual number of highly qualified candidates." Nor is anyone tactless enough to offer you a job and say, "Well, your teaching presentation was overly complex, but we liked you anyway." You just don't know; sometimes your potential employers don't either. The job hunt is not just about the objective catalog of your achievements. Many other subtle factors are at play, all to do with people and politics. That said, some things succeed or go awry in job hunting with enough frequency that they are worth considering before you even start scanning openings. The purpose of this chapter is to outline the commonly occurring human and political exigencies of the probationary faculty hiring process in higher education. Much of what follows will apply to and even be specifically written for

- those who have been working in temporary jobs for some time.
- assistant professors who may be thinking of switching tenure tracks or even applying for a position that might include P&T as one of its attractions.
- the ABD newly on the market.

Whatever your status, whatever your field, a fundamental truth is that while there are *good* jobs out there, no job necessarily includes every facet of a *perfect* job. Getting your first job or seeking new employment, thus, involves a bit of philosophizing as much as it does scanning the job ads in the *Chronicle of Higher Education* or the newsletter of your discipline, dressing appropriately for interviews, and avoiding typos in your letter of application. It would be wonderful if your initial posting turned out to be permanent and happy—that is, at the institution, in the locale, with the profile and contract, among the colleagues and students, and within the type of culture that you love and that fits your character and career orientation. As long as we are dreaming here, you get tenure and promotion and then promotion again in this wonderful place, and then you live out a long and satisfying career never thinking of looking elsewhere. Very few of us, however, enjoy such an idyll. There aren't many academics under the age of 40 who have not moved from at least one job to another. In sum, expect to travel. The first job does not have to be the final job.

## The Volunteerism Context in Academic Hiring

Technically you will be hired by an institution. In fact, you will be hired (or rejected, for that matter) by *people*. Does the search committee you are dealing with seem to be taking forever to do anything? Are your communications from them contradictory or at cross-purposes? Are they processing your application inefficiently? Are they inattentive or unknowledgeable when you ask questions? Is your campus visit a comedy of errors with mixed-up appointments and underattended presentations? An incompetent search may well signal a position that is an object of fierce contention, a complete lack of interest among the faculty, a department in disarray, or outright laziness and blockheadedness among your potential future colleagues. None of these conditions is attractive in any work environment, especially your tenure-track home. None, however, are uncommon for a reason that reflects the essence of the culture of the professoriate.

Here I recall some advice from my professor-father when I first started on the tenure track myself: he said that "you won't believe how much just filling out forms correctly and getting projects in on deadline yields a huge competitive advantage." Time and time again he has been proved right. In an average faculty member, you will discover a range of many positive qualities, but bureaucratic timeliness and acuity are not always among them. If you possess or develop good paperwork habits, you will help yourself prosper above and beyond many of your equally or more brilliant colleagues.

Search committees are a good example: a majority of searches are not well-oiled machines because the majority of faculty who run them are not trained or paid to make them so.[1] A faculty search is the functional equivalent of a church bake sale. Volunteers largely rule the roost, for good or bad. Unfortunately, the most brilliant physics professor and the most erudite English professor are essentially amateurs when it comes to the organization and the methods of headhunting and human resource management. Senior faculty have full-time jobs, and they may or may not think that a search is an intrinsic part of them. The search is probably not their first or even second daily priority . . . and so things slip, and time whiles by.

The volunteer context tends to result in the mixed-signal phenomenon of which job seekers often complain, especially popping up in campus visits. The dean tells you, "We are particularly looking for someone to help us with X," but the chair of the search committee insists, "We really like your work on Y," while a friendly senior faculty member offers the aside, "In your research presentation, make sure you bring up Z." It is possible that these people never got together and agreed on what they really wanted from the hire. Some of them, even members of the search committee, may have never read or may even disagree with the posted qualifications in the ad profile.

In such cases, rather than try to be a pretzel or present a different face to everyone, you should be true to the strengths and limitations of your own CV and interests, emphasizing how you fit the position as advertised, while also noting connections to the X, Y, and Z of individual preferences.

The point, however, is that these are people who are not trained headhunters, who are doing this voluntarily as extra work. Don't expect perfection; don't take mistakes personally.

## When to Go on the Market

If you are an ABD Ph.D. candidate who wants to work in academia, job hunting is necessary. The only real question before you begin looking for likely openings and putting together application materials is, Are you ready to go on the market? That decision is outside the scope of this book, but is one that should be made in partnership with your mentors and taking into account the particularities of employment in your discipline.

Two general caveats, however, for the doctoral student. First, a bureaucratic one: More and more post-doc and tenure-track positions demand that you have completed your degree by the time you begin work. "Completed" means completed—that is, defended and turned in for publication your dissertation. My present school, the University of Iowa, even requires that the graduate college at a new hire's doctoral institution write a letter certifying that all such work has been finished by the start date of the position.

Second, as mentioned in the chapter on doctoral education, mentors and advisers, however supportive and well-meaning, are not necessarily all-knowing, especially about job hunting. In context, a senior faculty member may have been last on the job market himself during the Carter administration. He may have only one or two students every two or three years looking for work. He may be in the later stages of his career and have dropped out of high-level publishing, attentive conferencing, and detailed networking. He may also like you, believe in you, and not want to discourage you from following the passion that, after all, he shares (or once shared). He certainly may not want to tell you, "Give up," or "The job market is just a disaster! You're in a lot of trouble." He may even be passing on out-of-date advice about writing a letter, formatting a CV, or the etiquette of the research presentation.

So listen to the seniors, but also read the *Chronicle of Higher Education* and *Inside Higher Ed,* and the field-specific blogs, wikis, and forums about the latest (and sometimes the worst) of what is happening today in the job market.

But *Promotion and Tenure Confidential* is also aimed at the tenure tracker who might want to switch rail lines—that is, to accept a position at another institution. So before we begin a unified analysis of seeking and applying for jobs equally relevant to anyone—not yet or already on the tenure track—I now offer a special discussion of job hunting while on the job. Seeking a different job as an assistant professor (or even as an associate) is tricky and nerve-racking, and may even undermine your career. Nevertheless, every tenure-track candidate should at least consider the option.

Let's begin with the initial decision to scope out possibilities on the job market.

**Are you feeling ethical qualms?** Many academics hesitate about switching jobs because they fear they are somehow letting down their colleagues, their students, and even their departments. They are fretting needlessly. I have changed jobs twice in my career. Both times I found new advisers for my students, someone else took over teaching my classes, and other faculty supervised my service projects. In other words, the university survived without me. Switching positions is also a recognized part of our profession. A professor once described how over the course of eight years working on his dissertation his entire initial committee had moved on or retired. If you handle the transition to a new institution well, it's unlikely your transfer will cause resentment or disruption.

**Have you assessed your current position and prospects?** Your reasons for wanting out of your current position no doubt vary. You may be at a rural campus, and your spouse can't find a job in the area. Support from your department may be insufficient for your growing research agenda. You may be incompatible with the senior faculty members. Or, most commonly, it is simply prudent to explore your options in the wider world. The essential question is: Are your local problems fixable or fundamental? If you hate your colleagues, your town, and the weather, no conceivable administrative intervention will heal your wounds. But if your current issues are resolvable, like a desire for new equipment in the lab, consider trying to work them out. The prospect of losing you may prompt improvements in your situation. *Beware the "quad is greener on the other side" phenomenon.* Academe, compared with many other professions, has a much more limited range of perks, privileges, and goodies for employees. If you feel undercompensated, make sure you can be rewarded in the way you want. On one campus a professor was purported to have complained regularly to his department chair that the university did not appreciate him. Each time, the unit attempted some sort of mollification. But over the years the dean wearied of the drama. He finally asked the professor, "What can I give you that will keep you happy and feeling valued forever?" The response was, "A car—a company car." Well, most institutions of higher learning cannot hand out Escalades to their professors, let alone Christmas bonuses or vacations to St. Moritz for top earners. The dean concluded that the professor was a lost cause.

In weighing your current rewards, make sure your comparisons are on the same scale. One scholar in economics nearly took another job because of its hefty pay bump but then turned it down after a cost-of-living calculation revealed that the more expensive area would nullify his increased income. In another case, an assistant professor switched jobs, enticed in part by a lighter teaching load. Unfortunately, he found the students were less academically prepared than were his previous ones, so his pedagogical labors actually increased.

**Are you aware of your time on the tenure clock?** The timing of an exit is a key factor. If you seek a new job a year or two after starting on the tenure track, people will wonder, "Why so soon?" You don't want to get a jumping-bean reputation. Switching too early also means that you have not had time to establish credentials that will improve both your job prospects and your contract deal. Few assistant professors are superstars a year out of their Ph.D. programs.

However, it is an individual's choice based on a particular situation. There is no optimum exit year because the tenure-track years, all of them, are your time of optimum mobility. Despite the enlargement and improvement over time of your CV, there will never be as many opportunities; depending on your personal circumstances, you may never be in a position to walk away for another position as easily as in those "virgin" years just out of the Ph.D. program. Moreover, that just-right job in the land of your dreams may come open this once; wait and it could disappear for decades. You can legitimately tell the search committee, "I couldn't pass up the possibility of working with you, and this position was not open last year when I took the job I have."

A less controversial exit point is within the one or two years before you go up for tenure. Regardless of whether you have been told that your tenure bid is all sewn up, looking for another job will allow for a back-up plan in the event your case turns out not to be a sure thing. You can explain to your colleagues, "I'd like to stay if you want me, but I also want to have a job, and nothing is certain." Late tenure-track job offers put you in a position to negotiate with strength—perhaps even for tenure itself. Alternately, if you get word that you are going to be denied tenure, an external job offer allows you to ask for the tenure process to be stopped, and then you can assert that you were never officially denied tenure—a very important distinction that I will elaborate on later in the chapter on the process of going up for tenure.

**Have you guesstimated your likelihood of success?** Normal hiring, as said, even when an institution expresses interest in your application, is full of intangibles. To navigate them, you need some help from trusted mentors. They can offer an appraisal of the job market and an assessment of how attractive a hire you are. Even then, hires of people are made by people and so are uncertain as human whims. You may be, according to every mentor and friend you have, a perfect fit for a position; but somebody else may be a finalist who, in the eyes of the search committee, is even more perfect.

A key element may be that, ready or not, now may be your only opportunity to move. In almost every field, the number of tenure-track positions open far exceeds those available for associate and full professors. Once I got tenure, for example, I joked that there were no more job openings for me the next year on planet Earth. I was about right: only one or two faculty positions at the associate or full rank fit my profile and my subfield and were not associated with administrative positions.

**What are your post-tenure prospects where you are?** A very successful researcher and administrator once pointed out that getting tenure someplace that you hate and being stuck there because of the lack of post-tenure mobility is more like a prison sentence than a good marriage. It is the equivalent, as she put it colorfully, to "three hots and a cot." Being an assistant professor on the tenure track is arduous. But it is wise to get some sense about what exactly is expected of you after tenure as well. On some campuses, resources for research will decrease and service loads will markedly increase. Perhaps you will get a modest salary bonus for tenure, but then you might watch as year after year the salary levels of the new assistant hires leap above the modest or non-existent "merit" increases for current faculty—the dreaded "compression phenomenon." You may decide that the last years of assistantship are also the last chances to significantly augment your salary, benefits, and contract goodies.

**Are you prepared for how much work the job search entails?** Success in employment-seeking should be balanced against the effort it takes. A true job search, in which you apply for numerous positions, is almost a part-time job in itself. How will your tenure-track progress be affected by the diversion of perhaps months and the commensurate concentration? One assistant professor spent so much time in his last two years on the tenure track looking for a job elsewhere that his productivity suffered. He came quite close to being denied tenure, and he never did find another position.

## Job Searching on the Job: Who Should Know?

If you seek another tenure-track job, the next issue to resolve is, Whom should you tell about your job search, and whom shouldn't you tell? If you don't think those are tricky questions, consider the following situations.

*Case 1:* An assistant professor who was satisfied with his institution, colleagues, and courses was nonetheless flattered when he got a call from a senior mentor at a more prestigious university encouraging him to apply for an opening there. By coincidence, the assistant professor met that day with his dean and mentioned the exchange. The dean said brusquely, "Well, I'm sorry to hear you are unhappy with us." From then on, the assistant professor felt that the administration had written him off as already gone when in fact he had just been musing aloud.

*Case 2:* An assistant professor increasingly dreaded the prospect of spending the rest of her life in a place and among colleagues she did not like. Worse, she and her department chair never seemed to click. At one point several of her peers suggested outright that she look for a job elsewhere. But she wondered: Won't it cripple my search if nobody internally will speak well of me?

*Case 3:* In her penultimate tenure-track year, an assistant professor was told by everyone, including her senior mentors, that her promotion was "a sure thing." Yet she knew there were no sureties in P&T, and that once she had tenure, her job options would shrink drastically. She decided to scan the want ads and apply for select positions. She told no one about her plans, not wanting her colleagues to think she was going to leave them just as they were considering her tenure case. But that put her in a quandary as to whom to list as internal references.

In short, the issue of whom to tell is complicated. So let's turn to how and why you should try to manage other people's awareness of your job search.

**Dealing with retaliation, resentment, and write-off.** Who knows how your potential or real job search can impact your career even if you stay put? The consequences of being seen as looking for an exit can be positive, negative, or both. Colleagues may resent you; students may feel hurt and potentially abandoned. Conversely, administrators may start to value you more and try to figure out how to keep you; or again, they may count you as a write-off.

A tenure-track faculty member at a small religious college recounted how, when it got around that he had interviewed for a job elsewhere, his colleagues started treating him "like an apostate." Even at a larger institution, you face the issue of resource allocation: if a dean thinks you have one foot out the door, will she be willing to accommodate your current requests?

**Keeping a low profile as a good investment.** The publicity factor in job hunting, especially when you are already on the tenure track, is a foggy terrain. As an assistant professor, I went on the market several times. I talked in confidence with a senior mentor who told me, "You have the right to explore your value; everyone does." True, but he also agreed that there were many levels of political subtlety about whom you should tell about your search, and what reasons you should give for looking to leave. Don't burn bridges you haven't crossed yet.

**Living in two worlds—town and gown.** A campus and the area it sits in can be small enough to warrant prudence when sharing details of your career plans. The academic discipline is a true global village, where people meet regularly at conferences, have long-standing friend-ships across continents, and engage in chat and gossip about events in the field via Facebook. In this era of instant global communication, you tell a colleague in Hong Kong or Bucharest about your job search, and the senior professor in the office next to yours may find out ten minutes later.

Likewise, in the town around the campus, people talk. You may confide in your neighbor, the pharmaceutical rep, who mentions your plan to a mutual acquaintance who is an insurance agent, and two weeks later your dean hears about your job search at a Rotary Club lunch. Even large and medium-size cities tend to have smaller groups of professionals who are involved in academic matters. You never know who is only a few degrees of separation from whom, so watch those loose lips.

**Making your confidentiality rules clear while understanding con-flicting loyalties.** I am always surprised by the number of faculty members who are job searching and don't clarify with their references the limits of who should know. An assistant professor at a small busi-ness college asked a colleague to serve as a reference but left the issue of confidentiality vague. To his horror, the senior professor brought up the younger man's job search at a faculty meeting. The intention was apparently innocent, even supportive, as in "We have to keep him." But consequently, other senior faculty members started acting as if he was a ghost: "They looked past me in the hallway!" It behooves you, then, to be precise in your request for silence about your employment explorations.

Yet one of the main problems with trying to restrict information about your job search is that nearly everyone you confide in will have conflicting loyalties. For example, you ask a senior faculty member to serve as a reference. She may well honor your request to keep confi-dence. But she may also be a member of the senior ruling group of the school, and a friend of the chair, and have mentees elsewhere whom she wouldn't mind applying for your job if you left. You have situated her where the sirens call for her to out you—perhaps discreetly, but to out you nonetheless.

There may be other circumstances in which a reference's interests and even ethics lead them to reveal your secret. For one thing, requesting that colleagues keep something in confidence does not translate as asking them to lie for you. If a dean or another faculty member hears a rumor that you are on the job market, don't expect your internal references to deny it if they are asked point-blank. Their relationship with other, tenured colleagues in the department is more important than their acquaintanceship with an assistant professor—who, after all, may be leaving.

**Discussing the confidentiality issue with search committees.** If you want confidentiality, you can ask for it. But remember the "volunteerism" context of faculty-run searches: these people are not CIA agents or ninjas. Yes, in theory and fact, there are ethical and legal rules and codes that govern searches. They are all routinely broken. In most cases, the reason is not malice but rather friendliness, incompetence, or inquisitiveness. A dean explained how she had instructed her faculty members—who had not conducted a search in years—on the exact human resources / equal opportunity and diversity (HR/EOD) rules for what questions could, and could not, be asked of candidates. Sure enough, several faculty members ignored her or didn't care and violated the protocols, as in, "So, do you have any kids?" or "Would you like to know about our local churches?" You should not count on everybody following the rules. You can ask search committees to keep your candidacy quiet, but it's never guaranteed.

**Keeping your job search from hurting your job.** Many assistant professors who are job hunting end up outing themselves. If you are aggrieved or desperate to escape your current job, it is easy to fall into the ethical and practical trap of sloughing off your current work in favor of your exit activities. We have all seen and heard of faculty members, especially assistant professors, who are so busy with their searches that they cut their own classes, blow off office hours, fail in service work, and generally act so distracted that they are hurting their departments and their own reputations. Even when you've told everyone why you are out of town or out of touch so much, they may rightly still resent you. Remember, job hunting is essentially something that you should be doing on your own time; it should interfere only minimally with your current teaching, research, and service obligations.

**Being careful of being "blogged out."** A young scholar accepted a position at another university. The process was smooth. The department asked him to apply, he sent in his CV, he visited, he accepted an offer, end of story. But a disconcerting sidebar was that he had been outed by anonymous postings on a Web site associated with his academic discipline. Someone had posted that he was interviewing for the position . . . before the interview even took place.

Welcome to the newest twist in the rapidly evolving world of online social networking. Now you can go to various blogs, Twitter feeds, and wikis and not only read news about openings but also find out who is interviewing or thinking about interviewing, whether an offer has been made and if it has been accepted. One such wiki brazenly asks for the cooperation of its gossip subjects by requesting, "Could those who have accepted offers please post the terms of your contracts, including initial salary offer and negotiated salary? Thanks." To which a commenter retorts—quite correctly—"In what *universe* is someone going to divulge this information in this way?"[2] While, as detailed later, social media can help the job search, they can also be dangerous to the candidate seeking cover.

Good old incompetence is the handmaid of the e-outing era as well. In late 2009, the wikis and blogs of the history discipline lit up with shock and guffaws when Johns Hopkins University's history department committed a mass outing, as described by the *Chronicle of Higher Education:*

> Academe is a small world, it's true, but you have reason to hope that your flirtation with another institution will fly under the radar of your colleagues, who will one day sit down to decide your tenure case (unless, of course, you actually happen to land a new job).
>
> So it is with horror that you open an e-mail update on the status of the search and realize that your email address and those of 105

others are visible for all of the applicants to see. The subsequent apology (bcc'd this time, of course) is cold comfort.[3]

All outings, intentional or not, are an ethical swamp that rivals the Okefenokee, but they have become a fact of job searching in academe. Everyone, especially tenure-track faculty members seeking new employment, should be well aware that their best-laid plans for secrecy may end up as gossip in the global Internet village of their field and their unit.

**Keeping too much secrecy from locking you out of a good reference.** There is such a thing as being too secretive. Job searches and speculation about applications are routine. The same chair who you worry will get mad at you for showing disloyalty may, in fact, be under consideration for a deanship elsewhere.

Then there is another curious but widespread phenomenon: even your worst enemy may become a friend when faced with the prospect of your exit. A young scholar had butted heads with an old bull on his faculty. The tussles became one factor that led the assistant professor to try to find more peaceful grazing elsewhere. To his surprise, his nemesis, on hearing of his search, volunteered to serve as an enthusiastic reference. The old fellow did not actually come out and say, "I'm happy to help you leave," but that was probably the motive.

At some point, of course, confidentiality dies a natural death—namely, when you are invited to a campus for an interview, or certainly when you receive an offer. You should be aware of the stages of the process. Know, for instance, when the search committee plans to start calling references, which is the most likely time that confidentiality will cease. Check out its policy about the level of publicity it gives an on-campus visit. It is common, for example, for institutions to put on their Web sites an announcement that someone is coming for an interview. I have even received such notices on e-mail discussion groups.

There are good reasons, when you are already on the tenure track and are considering switching to another job at another institution, for being prudent about whom you inform. Nevertheless, you may find that your guarded secret was common knowledge.

## Planning and Preparing for the Job Hunt: References

No one has ever sent in perfect application materials, nor met a job candidate who was ideal in every way. But the good job candidate with self-reflection, planning, and above all sensitivity will find ways to lessen chances of errors that might have major consequences for her job prospects.

Whatever your field, there will be different avenues for finding open jobs and applying for them. But some cross-disciplinary issues affect all application material and events.

First in line of importance is the letter of reference or personal reference (often via the phone but possibly also in e-mail or face-to-face). In many fields and for many job applications, one simply won't get hired or even considered without top references. But what constitutes a superior reference? For example, you are a doctoral candidate looking for a tenure-track job at a Carnegie "high-research" university. If you had a choice, would you want a letter of reference from a leading scholar in your field or one from a close friend of the head of the search committee? Or from a senior scholar who has not published in years versus from an assistant professor who is considered a rising star? How about a top researcher who was not on your committee and doesn't know you very well versus a not-very-prominent researcher who was your chair and has been your adviser for five years?

Here are some considerations for soliciting maximally effective "rec" letters:

**Carefully select your references, including those who are credentialed enough to make their praise count.** If you are sending out several applications, you may want to divide the references so that no one person is listed more than three times. That way no recommender will be overtaxed. Using more than one group of references also avoids putting all your hopes on one person's whims and persuasive abilities. (A doctoral student, however, must always list her adviser.) In general, the more status academics have in a field because of their affiliations and accomplishments, the more weight their words carry.

Repeating an observation made in the chapter on doctoral studies, however, the superstar reference can be a double-edged sword. It actually does happen in our business that a particularly renowned and powerful scholar can rig one of his students to get a job at another institution where he is respected, beloved, feared, or has pals (or former students) who are willing to do the favor or who are just excited about hiring an apostle of the genius. That you may be among the lucky ones in this situation should be balanced by the much larger number of people who are cut out of such jobs because rigging has taken place.

Conversely, know as well that you probably don't become renowned or respected without making enemies, either because of fights over research, politics, personal antagonism, or plain envy. In both of these situations, you hope someone—most especially your mentors—will give you some guidance. A young scientist described how his Great Man adviser went down a list of open positions and classified them into three groups: friends willing to give you a job, friends willing to look you over seriously, and enemies who will spit on you because you're my student.

**Help your references help you by summarizing and ranking applications.** When asking someone to serve as a reference, don't just say, "I'm applying for some jobs and need a reference" and leave it that. Give each reference a one-page summary of your applications. On that page, provide a brief description of each job you are seeking, and list some talking points about how well you fit the positions. (This is a good self-test of whether you do fit the jobs; if you can't persuade a reference, you won't be able to persuade a hiring committee, either.) Indicate the relative importance of each job by ranking the positions on your one-page summary in order from "most likely to accept if offered" to "least likely to accept." For written reference letters, the talking points may be especially helpful. If your recommender offers you the chance to read the letter of recommendation, take it. You care about your candidacy more than anyone else does, and you might find that some points are worth adding.

**Seek references who know you, not people who only know of you.**
References are almost always asked to "describe your relation or connections" to the candidate or applicant. The answer can negate or augment the value of the reference. A red flag shoots up when references
seem uncertain why they were asked to write a letter, as in "I learned
about Dr. Nemo's work when he asked me to support his candidacy."
Letters that misstate facts or omit obvious points are also quickly dis-
counted. One letter I saw misspelled the candidate's name and failed
to mention a teaching award she had received, although the writer referred in vague terms to her being a "great teacher."

**Choose references who can help contextualize flaws in your profile.**
In any application, it is good to deal with problematic issues that
someone might raise about you, or infer about your record, up front
rather than trying to cover up or make thin excuses. It is better when
your references help explain the context and augment your profile.
Take a typical example: an assistant professor trying to switch tenure-
track positions knows that her teaching evaluations for a particular
class are low or lower than her comfort level. The letter of reference
by her advocate is a great place to contextualize the problem: (a) it
was a methods course that students traditionally did not want or enjoy taking but was required and (b) that same semester, the instructor
had two new preps. The reference writer was able to further point out
that the scores increased in future evaluations for similar classes and
that the instructor had worked hard with the campus teaching center
to upgrade her pedagogy.

**Annotate the expertise of your references.** As described in the previous chapter, a particular mentor—and now reference—might be a true
and acknowledged expert in, say, research methodology. Rather than
having her include perfunctory praising of your teaching and collegiality, why not unleash her to expound at length on the cleverness,
creativity, and rigor of the methodology in your dissertation? Her expertise in that area will be, to use the military term, a "force multi-
plier." Search committees—who should recognize her credentials—
will react with something like, "Wow, this is high praise coming from

Professor Dayne!" Just make sure the reference explains her focus, as in, "I have not had a chance to supervise or witness Ms. Jackson teaching or being a TA, so here I will concentrate on her research accomplishments and potential."

**Remind your references.** Remember, your references may not be called for months. If you hear that a hiring committee will soon be contacting them, remind your references and resend the list of talking points. One senior biology professor recounted how he received a phone call late on a Friday afternoon from the head of a search committee who said they were checking the references of a finalist for a position. The professor only vaguely remembered that there were some important talking points for this particular institution to fit the profile of the ideal candidate but had forgotten what they actually were. He stumbled through the reference call, saying positive things but sensing that they weren't the exact positive notations that would have best helped his protégé. Help your references help you.

## Job Application Items: Step by Step

The job application is a collection of materials that vary from discipline to discipline, from institution to institution, and from position to position. Nevertheless, many have standard components and also common people and politics challenges.

**Letter of inquiry or application.** A head of a social sciences unit described a job application letter that his department received that ran to nearly a dozen pages of autobiographical and philosophical meandering. The purpose of a letter of inquiry for an academic job is to notify formally the search committee that you are applying for an advertised position and to describe how you fit it. The document should be concise; once you go beyond a few pages of self-description for an assistant professor position you are bordering on lexical obesity. On the other hand, you can be too laconic: I once got a letter that said simply: "My materials are attached."

You want significant items to stand out like skyscrapers on a plain but avoid overdoing self-praise. If, for example, you won a teaching award as a doctoral student, say so, and even add some context like that the award only goes to one person a year and is voted on by both faculty and undergraduates. Don't embellish by adding that "everybody congratulated me for winning the award." The search committee will hear such praise from its proper source, your laudatory references.

**Teaching philosophy.** No single item on a checklist of job application materials causes as much confusion and anxiety as the statement of teaching philosophy. I recall my own first attempt to craft one as painful and stilted; what could I write that was high-minded enough to qualify as a "philosophy"? Again, the best approach is to weigh the goals of the document, to show that you have thought about teaching, that you hold ideals and apply tactics to teaching that fit the pedagogical reality and aspirations of the target institution. Principles and practicality should not conflict. Although it is fine to assert, "I believe every student deserves my personal attention," someone on the search committee might reasonably ask, "In 500-student lecture classes as well?"

In contrast, an excellent statement of teaching philosophy for one humanities applicant is a good example of what to do right. She affirmed succinctly how she wanted to make sure each student had the "best possible" classroom experience but placed it in the context of feasibility. She then enumerated how she prepared for new classes, how she organized the lesson plan, and how she graded. She was communicating to the committee that (a) she understood that for their institution, a research university, teaching was one component of the expectations for her professional success and (b) she did not feel she was a perfect teacher but treated her "philosophy" as flexible. She cited some examples of failed assignments and described how she rectified them in the next iteration. She came off as someone who took teaching seriously but not arrogantly or obsessively, which matched the culture of the target department.

**Curriculum vitae.** The format may vary by field, and even by institution; a good baseline is online CVs of search committees. But the actual content is guided by two rules of restraint. First, CVs are not a collection of Twitter tweets by a reality television show "star." You do not need to document every event in your life. I have seen CVs stuffed with the topic of each class lecture, hobbies, (nonacademic) travels, pets, and even political philosophies. Interesting? Perhaps. Irrelevant? Absolutely. The search committee wants to know about your teaching history, your conference presentations, your publications, and so on. Don't bury such details in a forest of other material.

Second, the CV is a list of facts, not a propaganda tract. If you, as a doctoral student, designed a new course—an unusual achievement— just list it under a header of "New Courses Designed." Don't annotate with descriptions of all the effort expended. That can be mentioned in passing in your letter and expounded upon in detail by your references. Likewise, there is no need to say that you are well published; listing your publications is sufficient, as the search committee can and will count them and estimate their quality, impact, and venues.

**Research presentation.** I first realized how a job candidate can overdo a research presentation when I was a doctoral student. The applicant was poised and polished—indeed, overwhelming, but not in a good way. His PowerPoint showed slide after slide of dense, micro-fonted verbiage about a study that he described in Gatling-gun narration. He packed a six-hour lecture into 60 minutes, leaving about 30 seconds for questions. I felt vertigo from all the graphs and bullet points flitting by. He was so eager to showcase his work that he forgot a research presentation is not only about research but also about *presenting*: proving you have the ability to speak to groups of peers about your work clearly, concisely, and within constraints of legibility and time. More is not better.

An overdone research presentation will undermine your job application in another way if you are a Ph.D. student. Search committees, faculties, and unit heads will question, "Will she finish her dissertation in time to start the job?" Be overlong, overly complex, too wide-ranging, or overambitious, and the impression will be, "Compelling, impressive, but no way will she finish by August!" Even a tenure-track assistant professor interviewing for another job may undercut his chances by hyperinflating the research presentation. The audience will wonder, "Can he keep up his research program? Will it lead to enough quantity and quality publications for tenure?" Blast the room with a massive plan of stratosphere-reaching efforts, and the reaction might be, "I don't think he can pull it off and get tenure."

**Teaching presentation.** The teaching presentation also should be approached by determining what are its goals and who is the audience. Your objective is to communicate that you are in command of material that you will probably be teaching in your new department, that you can establish and maintain a good rapport with students, and generally that you seem to be an organized and competent pedagogue. Your audience comprises both students and faculty.

Here, too, you can do too much or too little. A doctoral student had a series of handouts for the class he was presenting in as part of a campus job visit that amounted to several hundred pages per student. Unsurprisingly, his PowerPoint clocked a hefty hundred slides or more. In another case, an assistant professor applying for a tenure-track job was so eager to show off his brilliance that his high leaps of theory and dense statistical analysis flummoxed the undergraduate intro class to which he was presenting. He convinced the committee that he was indeed a smart fellow but also a poor teacher. Conversely, barely getting through ten minutes when you have an hour-long class to teach or seeming to run out of ideas or thoughts will convince the committee that you would not be able to master a single class day, let alone a semester.

**Interviews.** Having nothing to say at an interview is fatal. But overdoing it can manifest itself in interviews, lunch conversations, and drop-in chats, whether at conferences, on the phone, or during campus visits. It is damaging to be over-rehearsed, to answer every question like a politician at a debate who has memorized a stock response and can't depart from his talking points. Reciting is not talking, and interviews are about showing you can listen as much as proving you can speak. Beware prolixity as well. If you have a fifteen-minute interview at an academic conference, taking fourteen minutes to answer the question "What is your dissertation about?" will not leave anyone awed, only dulled into daydreaming.

The last component of application materials and events, the job interview, is a crucial enough encounter and one so tied to the "people and politics and personal" issues of careers that it is worth exploring in depth.

## Interviewing for the Hire

You apply for a job . . . and you receive a call! Sometimes a committee will want to prescreen applicants through a phone question-and-answer. Professional conferences constitute the most common setting for brief, fast-paced, face-to-face interviews. Then, of course, you might be invited to visit the campus. Whatever the setting, some basic principles apply.

**Personalize.** Good interviewees figure out a way to make interviewers feel vested in the success of the exchange. Arrive at an academic job interview as informed as you can be, not only about the institution, the unit, and the requirements of the position but also the people to whom you will be talking. Structure your style, the content of your questions, and even your manner to fit the particular audience.

The single best interviewee I ever saw for an assistant professor position showed up with a set of elaborate notes, print-outs, and materials organized around every person she was scheduled to talk to and practically every other occupant of our school. She had even looked up on the Web the individual accomplishments of our grad students and was able to speak about their research interests and projects. For senior faculty, she had printed out copies of several of their published papers, complete with highlights and marginalia questions. We were impressed and convinced that the intention was not flattery—although I admit we were flattered—as much as demonstrating her considerable interest in our position. One member of our search committee mused, "Did she go overboard in the prep? Probably, but she is really trying to get this job. You have to be impressed with that." Indeed, she displayed more than just a generic need to be employed. She showed that she cared about and wanted to work with us. She was hired.

**Know your audience.** Heed one of the oldest lessons of politics: Although you don't need to baste your audience, you must talk to them in the language they understand about the issues that concern them. For example, if you are interviewing for a position at a professional or liberal arts or community college, practically every audience you will deal with wants to hear about how much you enjoy teaching, your dedication to teaching, and your experience and skills in teaching.

You can get a fairly good sense of people's interests and concerns from online biographies or CVs or your own research through contacts who know something about the department. A professor concerned about declining teaching standards, for example, probably has written on the subject. Find and read what he has written. If you are having lunch with him, bring it up and showcase your pedagogical credentials. The point is not to twist yourself into someone who promises everything to everybody but to make sure that each constituency for your job prospects feels her or his concerns are adequately addressed.

When you are actually facing your audience is when you also need to gauge the room. Among the common complaints about job candidates in general, regardless of the field, is that they are too focused and rehearsed. They fail to listen to the queries and responses from the search committee and others they meet at professional conference interviews, on the phone, and during campus visits. In terms of warding off possible objections to your candidacy, use your senses to measure individuals you meet and those you address with presentations. You want to detect—good listeners hear tone as well as words—if something you have said (or left unsaid) has anyone wondering, perplexed, or even irritated.

For example, a social science assistant professor, looking to switch from one tenure-track job to another, was invited for a campus interview. At the initial dinner with the search committee, someone asked him about his research interests. His answer was polished and comprehensive. He could tell, however, that one senior faculty member looked a bit disconcerted. That night, back at the hotel, the candidate did what he should have done earlier and looked over the old fellow's CV. He found that in the early part of his career the senior scholar had published extensively in a related area.

The next day, when the candidate met his possible nemesis he made it a point to bring up how his own research was connected to some of the senior man's work. The effect was palpable; the senior scholar was mollified and was more genial through the rest of the interview visit. Of course there is balance here as in all aspects of impression management; you shouldn't look needy or like a loafer-licker.

**Take notes as an aid to responding but also as a sign of respect.** An interview is an exercise in conversation and mutual learning. If you spent the whole interview just answering questions, you haven't done a good job. On the other hand, if you spent an entire interview probing the representatives of the search committee (or whomever you are speaking with), you probably will not have made a good impression.

A tool for improved interviewing—that is, an interview that is considered successful by all parties involved—is to use a notepad and pen. It is an unfortunate trend among students today, even graduate students perhaps too reliant on iPods and instant messaging, that they will show up at someone's office to ask complicated questions and either don't take notes or ask for pencil and paper as an afterthought. Taking notes is not just about the accumulation of knowledge but is also symbolic of caring about what the conversation partner says. Showing up with a notepad and taking appropriate notes during an interview communicates the following:

- What the search committee members or others representing the school are saying is important to you.
- The information they are giving you will be retained when you work with them.
- You are a professional: organized, thoughtful.

Just make sure taking notes does not interfere with the discussion. Cross-talk peters out when people see only the top of your head. They may even restrict their comments if they feel they have to slow down so that you can record everything verbatim. It is also polite to ask permission to take notes. If you perceive someone letting you in on something secret—a bit of gossip, or an insider disclosure—stop writing.

**Ask questions.** Sometimes the only way to know if you have failed to say enough or have said too much on a subject is to ask. Query your interviewers to the effect of, "If I were lucky enough to be working with you, what would be your advice about priorities?" Such a question expresses a degree of humility that is always an attractive quality in a young scholar. It also is open-ended and inviting so that someone who genuinely may have that proverbial bee in her bonnet about one issue in the hiring profile will expose it and allow you to address it.

Follow up on faculty questions and major points with questions of your own that register your interest and intelligence. A political scientist described a job visit by a candidate whose CV promised intellectual credentials that were quite strong but proved to be a disappointment in person. A senior professor in the department asked him at the end of his research presentation a friendly but provocative question about another strain of research (hers) that might converge with his own. The candidate's answer, "Yeah, I'll think about that one." The professor pressed on, "Are there any questions you want to ask me about the relationship of these two bodies of research?" His answer: "No, I got it." The senior scholar later related her dissatisfaction at the search committee meeting: "He seems to lack intellectual curiosity. Maybe he forgets we're hiring an assistant *professor.*" They didn't hire him.

You also have an opportunity to probe seriously about the position itself. A conversation starter is, "In what role do you see this hire in the future development of the program?" If you get very similar positive and illuminative answers from everybody, it is a good sign that the unit has agreed on not only the criteria for hire but the expectations for P&T. If they offer wildly divergent answers, it is a warning sign that you might be contorted in different directions by people who cannot agree on what they hope you will become on the job.

**Deal with deal-breakers.** The trickiest kinds of questions are on what might be for you or for them the "deal-breaker" issues. Suppose, for example, there was no minimum salary listed. One communications studies doctoral candidate described traveling for a campus visit, really hitting it off with the committee and chair, but then finding out during the exit interview that the salary would be much lower than he had expected. Well, that's the kind of question that probably should have been dealt with even before a campus visit—as in, what is the range of salary? Here, however, is one of those conundrums that does not have a universal solution. I have heard faculty and chairs express that they didn't like it when previsit candidates started inquiring about salaries early in the process. As one dean put it, "First job offer, then salary." Here is where you hope you might have a friend or strong partisan on the inside who can give you a hint about either the salary level or the culture of acceptability of asking about the salary level.

The grandest deal-breaker of them all, the one that has always been a sensitive area in academic hiring—even more so in difficult economic times—is the spousal accommodation. A young arts scholar once asked me, "I'm going on an interview and I think I'm a strong candidate, but I would only accept the position if they found something for my wife in her own field. Do I bring that up?" I have seen definitive answers posted in job advice columns, wikis, blogs, and forums that go in either direction: "No, don't bring it up; wait until they offer a job and then negotiate" or "Yes, bring it up early. They will get the hint and you will be able to gauge the possibilities of spousal accommodation by their reaction."

In times of dire funding constriction, it may simply not be possible to accommodate your spouse or partner, so if you sound like it is a true deal-breaker, the deal will be broken immediately—they won't offer you a job. That is why it is extremely important for academic couples to seriously consider the possibility of not demanding mutual appointments. Remember, just because you start apart doesn't mean that a few years down the road there might not be a way for you to be together both professionally and in location. Talk through your plans now, or you and your partner may have to make uncomfortable last-minute decisions later.

**Deal with inappropriate questions . . . and perhaps turn them to your advantage.** You are a doctoral candidate and have been invited for an on-campus interview for an assistant professor position at an institution where you would love to work. At the get-acquainted dinner, the hiring committee's talk focuses on children, K–12 schools, the best place to hold an 8-year-old's birthday party, and the sought-after babysitters on campus. One of the committee members turns to you and asks, "So, do you have children?" In fact, you have two little ones at home, and you are very interested in information about local schools and the child-friendliness index of the town because accepting the job, if offered, is a family commitment, not just a professional decision. But you wonder whether too much kid talk at this stage will overshadow your attributes as serious scholar and teacher. And isn't asking about your personal life not allowed? What is the proper response?

Probably no topic has been of greater contention on online academic jobs forums than what to do when a candidate is asked a question that is ethically and/or legally inappropriate. Again, there is no one-size-fits-all response. Individuals and situations vary. Do you think, for example, that the inappropriate question was asked maliciously, innocently, or inadvertently? Do you care whether they know the answer or not? How badly do you want the job? One important context: Although faculty who ask inappropriate questions are breaking rules of their own university, unless they do so with outrageous flagrancy, the chances that they will be punished and you will be offered a position are about zero. (For serious violations of discrimination laws, however, there are lawsuit and EOD complaint options; an attorney experienced in higher education litigation can counsel you.) As stated earlier in this book, very few tenured faculty members are dismissed "for cause" each year; I have never heard of one who has been fired for bad search committee technique.

So, in the case above, I would not advocate testiness or a strongly worded retort, as in, "That's an illegal question; it's none of your business." Nor should you completely ignore the question, as in staring at them blank-faced, looking down at your salad, or crunching noisily on a carrot. A more shrewd and tactful response might be something like, "Yes, I have two daughters, and both of them are already interested in science. It's quite gratifying. They completely understand the long hours I need to put in at the lab." In other words, turn the question back to your talking points for the position. Remember that other people in the room, especially if you are asked this question at a larger session, are probably groaning at the ineptness of their colleague and will credit you for your gentle yet clever response.

In another case, a professor of biochemistry described an especially deft job candidate who, upon being barraged with family-related questions by a clueless search committee member, turned the situation to her advantage. She related how her children were fascinated by her research and how she had volunteered at their school to demonstrate science projects. The committee was duly impressed by her dedication to work but also her evangelization of their field. It was an instance of making "family" work for the job candidate.

Finally, a situation where *you* want to bring up family as a topic is when the search committee thinks it's a positive. In small rural schools, the faculty may worry that "unconnected" newcomers will find their social lives too barren and will thus seek a position elsewhere. One such college's English department could not retain anyone who did not grow up in that part of the country or who was not already married. Ultimately, those conditions became unwritten qualifications for the hire; the search committees, often through snooping conducted by the real estate agent or grad students, determined to find out whether the job prospects could "fit here." Illegal? Yes, but also practical because the people who did not "fit" found working there unfulfilling and tried to get out as soon as they could.

**Limit pontifications and rambling.** A mistake that novice job seekers make in trying to avoid antagonizing anyone is to be too cautious and cryptic. The impression left, instead, may be that you are too timid for the classroom and too detached for the lab. On the other hand, we have all witnessed, and not a few of us have actually engaged in, the "worldly philosophical" job talk. In one such instance, the candidate discussed his research area, which was pretty much limited to a single entertainment television program. But every question, and every PowerPoint graphic, prompted rambling discourses on many issues, political, sexual, and social. There did not seem to be a topic under the sun that the fellow did not touch on or presume expertise. One member of the search committee speculated that the candidate, if asked to teach the intro course, would need four years to complete one semester. Stay on topic and on message.

**Avoid arrogance; point out your own flaws.** No matter what a doctoral candidate or assistant professor trying to switch tenure-track jobs has accomplished, arrogance is never appropriate or attractive. Remember that pretty much everyone who will vote on your hire is your senior, at least in age if not achievement. The more cocksure and self-important the image you present, either in your letter or in person, the more likely someone will find a reason to reject you at the next search committee meeting. Don't come off as thinking "I am too good for you." A famous interchange in Akira Kurosawa's film *Seven Samurai* (1954) offers some advice. The samurai defending a peasant village from a gang of bandits detect a weak spot in the village's fortifications. One, however, notes, and I paraphrase, "Every good fortress should have some obvious gap so that we know where the enemy will attack." For instance, a search committee might actually prompt you to reflect upon your own abilities when they ask at a teaching session something like, "What are your biggest challenges in the classroom?" or "What areas of pedagogy would you like to improve the most?"

The answer can show both your lack of braggadocio and your solution-oriented spirit. A Ph.D. candidate interviewing for a position, when asked this question, replied that the first time she taught a class she made the mistake of assuming that the students remembered everything from the prerequisite course. The outcome was that she got three or four weeks into her course and then had to backtrack when it became clear that most of the students hadn't remembered much from the on-the-books prereq. Now, she spends "the first class of the semester reviewing key terms and concepts, and I create an initial assignment where I ask them to go back and resurrect a major insight of the prereq." The committee was duly impressed by the adaptability of the young woman. She didn't just teach; she thought about teaching.

Another superb job candidate, while presenting her dissertation research, recounted several mistakes and the lessons learned from them. I think everybody in the room felt that her "failures" put her in a positive light. At the same time, she deftly demonstrated that her solutions were efficacious enough that there was no worry that she would finish her dissertation on time to take a job. Here was someone who learned from errors, grew, and did better—a process for which, after all, the tenure track is intended.

## Asking about the Status of the Search

One anonymous poster on an academic jobs wiki in early 2010 cried out: "AAAaaaaaaaaah! What is taking them so long!? It's April next week and I'm still waiting on 5 apps. How much longer does this go? . . . This is horrible. The waiting and the silence."[4] The job seeker was not alone. Far and wide candidates wonder: "What is the status of the search?"

The news may be bad, but for many people confirming a failed job application is the mental analog of ripping off a Band-Aid: better to get the pain over with quickly. Closure delayed is anxiety prolonged. The "enforced passivity" of waiting, to borrow a phrase from historian Robin Fedden, while others decide your fate, is maddening. Doing something active, like a status inquiry or even indirect snooping, makes you feel empowered, however slightly.

In a practical vein, there are good reasons to know the status of your job search as soon as possible. Finding out that you did not get a position is useful if you divine in it a trend or pattern. In job hunting, unfortunately, many seekers follow the wholesale approach, sending out applications for every job, even those for which they are patently unsuited. Search committees confronting several hundred applications will almost never choose someone who only marginally fits the position. If you are consistently getting turned down in a particular subfield, it may be an indication to give up on it.

On the other hand, the status check is required when you have received a job offer. Do not hesitate: The moment you get notification, start calling the chairs of every search committee of other departments at which you have applied. (At this point, you can cull out your "plan d" and "back-up" schools.)

Your message should be clear and concise. You have received another offer and want to notify them. Only add "you are my first choice" if they really are. If you have a certain amount of time to respond—like the typical two weeks—say so. Maybe nothing will happen, but you will certainly find out how excited they are about your candidacy. If you have already conducted a campus visit and interview, the situation becomes truly intriguing. Were you their number-one pick but they simply haven't gone through the campus bureaucratic process toward producing an offer? Then, you will be in that most delightful of situations, with multiple paramours vying for your affection.

What about the true "what's up" fishing expedition, when there is no offer in hand? In the 1990s and before, when applications were submitted by paper mail, it was perfectly acceptable to "check in" to "make sure all materials had arrived." Later in the process you could use the excuse of "sending an updated CV" as a reason to call a search chair and chat, which might lead to a brush-off, an "I can't share that information with you," or who knows, a connection and an interview.

Today, many universities employ Web sites where all materials, from writing samples to letters, are posted and allow you to confirm delivery yourself. Some lock you out after the initial submission process, however, so you can still try the "update my CV" gambit as an intro to the search chair.

Now, what if you have no excuse at all but curiosity and worry? Unfortunately, a simple inquiry is not so simple. There are departments and individuals who don't like the status question, although if they get irritated with you on the phone, perhaps they weren't championing your candidacy in the first place.

The situation has been made worse by the pressures of the modern job hunt. For many positions, there are more candidates, more anxious than ever; in turn, search committees are facing bigger burdens of processing and selection. One inquiry phone call or e-mail is no trouble, but forty will tax committees who are, after all, volunteers.

In addition, search chairs can get frustrated and flummoxed by inquiry calls and e-mails because they can't, rather than won't, respond. There are human resources and privacy issues about being too forthcoming regarding a search committee's activities. Committees certainly cannot tell you whom they just made an offer to until it's officially accepted and all the contracts have been signed and approved.

Search committees may also not be fully revealing because the tactics of searching demand such. It is theoretically possible, for example, that all three finalists may not work out, and a search committee might start looking for additional candidates to interview. Telling an inquirer, "We have our top three; they are coming to campus next week," might sabotage that process.

There are two solutions to avoiding a direct status check that might result in alienating the search chair. The first is old-fashioned backdoor inquiry, human to human. The second takes advantage of new media.

In the old days, as today, you could and can get a sense of the culture of the search committee or even glean what is going on in the search from insider contacts. As discussed in the previous chapter, Ph.D. students should build a friendly network of doctoral students in other programs during their years of study, especially in programs where they might one day think about applying. Nobody will be a better source of gossip about a search or more likely to leak information.

Modern online social media also allow avoidance of the angst of the ask. Job wikis, forums, and blogs present an intelligence system that focuses on your discipline where you can read that "three finalists have been invited to campus," "the search committee has made its recommendation but the department chair is sitting on it," or "they just hired someone, but the contract negotiations are dragging out." Web-based interactive venues, however, have several drawbacks as search-status monitors. First, they may be erroneous, perhaps even intentionally so. A rumor posted on the Web is no more or less reliable than one passed on by phone, although the former does allow people with contradictory postings to pass on their information, too. Sometimes, allegedly, postings constitute misinformation, actual attempts to discourage additional applicants to a position by spreading the word that "they plan to hire an insider" and "they already have their top three picked."

Social media also are controversial for search committees. To paraphrase a senior professor who discovered extensive wiki reports on the search he was leading, "It's ridiculous! We go to great lengths to maintain confidentiality and people are airing our every move!" He does not represent a minority opinion. If you are going to post information to a job wiki, be careful to leave out any truly identifying details. Be aware, for example, that some sites reveal your i.p. address. Depending on how many applications a department has received, merely posting from your campus computer, or even a computer in your city, may "out" you.

In all, job seeking in academe, especially when you are a graduate student or untenured, is never a serene journey. Too much information, especially when it is contradictory, can be as disconcerting as too little. But the status check inquiry, whatever trepidations you feel about the act, sometimes is necessary for you to move on in your mind as well as in the practical task of focusing on other openings.

## Deciding Whether to Accept a Job Offer

In the P&T process, the single most important hurdle is getting that first full-time, tenure-track job. Similar angst sometimes attends deciding whether to *take* a job offer, especially if the position is less than ideal because of its demands, institution, or locale. How do you decide whether to accept or decline a position? How much do you have to negotiate?

All the considerations assume that you have a choice. If you must pick between a mediocre first job in a part of the country you loathe among people you don't respect versus playing a conga drum on a subway platform, then sign that contract. However, even students in fields where jobs are scarce lament that they said yes without waiting for other applications to bear fruit, or before taking a further year to spruce up a CV and look for another opening—or at least without being more thoughtful about their contract negotiations.

One of the great advantages of academia over many other types of employment is that research, teaching, and service allow us to study and express our passions and be paid for the endeavor. Most of the rest of humanity does not have this opportunity. An academic job, thus, should be judged by multiple attributes, ranging from income to location to the status and reputation of the institution to our own cultural affinities. Each of these variables is not as hard and fast as some people assume: "salary" means more than just take-home income; "teaching load" means more than the number of courses taught per semester or academic year; "research profile" means more than how many big-name scholars are on the faculty.

**Salary and benefits.** For those of us who lived for years on student stipends, one-semester teaching stints, and serving as human subjects for medical trials, the prospect of a real salary with benefits is an oasis in a desert. Raw numbers, though, are misleading. A young friend e-mailed his delight about getting a good job with a "great" salary at a respectable college. The question he failed to ask himself was how far that salary would go in a major northeastern city. Two years later, he accepted a job at a college in a southern town with a low cost of living for less take-home pay. Rates of rent, home prices, taxes, and commuting costs all factor in; you should assess them.

A further consideration is the bewildering world of medical benefits, to which unmarried, childless 27-year-olds tend to pay almost no attention. Some institutions or their health insurance providers are unforthcoming about the coverage of chronic conditions. One health plan at one school may offer such coverage, while another plan at another college may not. Salary differences between the two, at that point, would become moot. An assistant professor whose spouse has a chronic medical condition requiring expensive monthly treatments explained, "For me, it's all about the medical plan's policy on preexisting conditions and how much they pay for [the particular] treatment. Salary is secondary."

Force yourself, as well, to review the retirement plan. What is their contribution versus yours? Over forty years of a career, a few percentage points either way will make a gigantic difference. The same is true for annual pay increases. Future projections, unless you will be working under a union contract, are difficult to make, but what are the historical increases or lack of them?

And, of course, examine benefits for a spouse or partner, even if you don't have one at the time of your hire. In all, you might be surprised after calculating for cost of living what the true wages of a position are.

**Teaching load.** Almost every institution of higher learning has a version of an allocation-of-effort contract that defines the proportions of research, teaching, and service expected of you. In terms of teaching, just as often it will be part of your contract that you will, say, teach a 2-2 or 3-3 or 4-4 load. Sometimes the split is specified as across two semesters; other times it is a projection of units across a year. So, for example, if a college class is designated as three units, a 3-3 teaching load might be written up as 18 units over the course of an academic year.

There are nuances below the surface, however:

- Teaching a course with which you are familiar is quite different than teaching a "new prep," especially in those initial semesters on the tenure track.
- The ratio of graduate versus undergraduate classes matters, as do seminars as opposed to "101" classes.
- What is the department's stance on buying yourself out of teaching a class with grant money?
- Is there a possibility of "flex loading," when your department reduces your teaching to help you focus on some other part of the job, like research publication?
- Are there anticipated changes in post-tenure course loads?

**Nonsalary support.** A particularly aggressive young assistant professor asked for a reserved parking spot as part of his start-up deal; he was denied. I do not recommend such demands unless you already have that MacArthur genius grant or Templeton Prize in hand. But a remarkable number of items can fall under the heading of support. Many just-about-to-be-hired faculty think only about research funds, grad assistants, travel money, or even lab space, but the list extends much farther, from furniture to spousal accommodation. Sometimes a small shift in the wording of the contract item can make a big difference. A STEM researcher got in writing that she could choose her post-doc assistant from the pool of possibilities, not just accept what the graduate director assigned her. She found it exceptionally helpful for her work that she did not have to stand in line behind senior faculty for the best candidates.

**Academic culture.** An assistant professor once described the atmosphere of the tiny liberal arts college that gave him his first job. Students and faculty hung out together at football games and tailgate parties. The faculty themselves were without any rivalries: jovial, easygoing, and supportive of each other. The administration was decentralized and strived to create a climate of genial governance and transparency. It was one big happy family.

He hated it all. What he loved instead was high pressure, competition, hierarchy, and anomie.

In other words, while there are objectively "bad" and "good" places to work in our trade, often the difference is in the psyche of the beholder. It is vital, then, to appraise the culture of your target institution. But don't expect to get an accurate picture just by asking. Certainly request to see the official document that describes a unit's P&T requirements but also ask what is their record of granting P&T. During the interview process, faculty tend to be less than candid about internal troubles.

Some cues of collegiality: Do they seem to be friendly to each other during the interviews? Are their office doors closed even when they are in? Do they publish together? Alternately, when someone tells you, "We are at war with each other," he might just be a disgruntled outlier (or an outright liar). Cultures also change. The retirement of a single powerful éminence grise or the stepping down of a dean can alter the atmosphere and ways of business of a whole unit.

**Locale.** One of the major criteria that many first-timers use to rate a possible job opening favorably or unfavorably is location: rural versus urban, far from versus close to family and friends, or tropical versus quasi-polar climate. As in the case of the small-town-hating scholar previously mentioned, if you truly believe that a particular environment will drive you batty, don't go there. Remember that one of the three Ps is *you*—will your personality fit this place? But consider putting up with a high level of dissatisfaction in this category if the trade-off is for a good position, one that launches your career rather than stultifies it. Again, a starting station need not be a final destination.

And you never know whether you might grow fond of an area that didn't attract you in prospect. My first job was in a place and with a culture alien to my own but offering the delights of food and friendship. Urban-oriented young faculty sometimes contend that they are rather glad to find themselves someplace like a small town where there are few distractions from hard and focused work. As one bucolic burg-dweller put it, "If I had gotten a job in Los Angeles, I don't think I'd be getting tenure."

**Management.** Your possible new unit will have a head: a chair, director, or dean, the person who is directly responsible for hiring you, who calls you to offer the position, who negotiates with you on your contract. You will have heard something about him or her from faculty and may have an existing impression based on his or her reputation in the field. Almost certainly, you met this person at an entrance or exit interview. Will you get along with your new boss? Do you want to work for him or her?

The reason why this is less decisive a factor in choosing whether to accept an academic position than for, say, a salesperson at a car dealership is that in higher education faculty management or administration is somewhat ambiguous. (More on this in the next chapter.) Your chair or director or dean will indeed have a great deal of power over your progress in many areas, from salary increases to committee assignments. But in academia there is a range of other people, such as the sitting members of the P&T committee and your faculty mentors, who can alternately be supportive of or disruptive to your career.

Furthermore, heads come and go, sometimes very rapidly. A junior faculty member recalled that since his department rotated chairs every three years and he was hired in the last year of one, he was now about to go up for tenure under his third chair. The problem was that the initial one had made some off-the-book promises of support, long forgotten and never fulfilled. Worse, chair number 3 loathed chair number 1, and the tenure tracker felt that the former would not be upset if a hire made by the latter failed to get tenure.

Relationships evolve as well. The friendly dean working so hard to recruit you may grow indifferent once you have complained too much about your teaching schedule. She has dozens of other faculty to please, most of whom have more power than you do.

**Status and reputation.** One of the reasons the school's reputation and support for you are more important in your first job than location or environment is elitism, the least challenged prejudice of the academy. Elitism often trumps all other kinds of "isms." In any field, you can look up national rankings. Sometimes a unit will be ranked by a straight number, as in "23rd in the country"; sometimes it will be within groupings, like "2nd tier."[5] The prestige of a program is much more stable than its roster of faculty. It is often said that it takes ten years to gain a reputation in academia and ten years to lose one, so delve into the current status of a program in the wider field rather than accepting an Internet listing.

Reputation can also have unanticipated or even inverse effects, depending on the discipline and the school to which you are applying for your first job after getting your doctoral degree. If you want to end up at an Ivy League school, obtaining your degree from an Ivy League school is a good start. Universities tend to hire at their peer level or above, not below.[6] An example of this can be seen in the degree bylines of the "core" faculty of Yale University's American Studies program as of 2008: almost every one is from an Ivy League, near–Ivy League, or Big 10 institution, and all have top reputations as *major research universities.*[7] In some fields, a few programs serve as feeders for the hiring of the majority of faculty at other top programs.[8] There is a strong caste system in academia, as the research on the subject and the obsessions with rankings demonstrate.[9]

As a result, when you are selecting a target program, you should do a little detective work on the issues behind and beside the headlined numbers. A unit and an institution have ratings tied to their name that may or may not accord with their actual achievements. The status of the name Harvard University, for instance, is so elevated that in the past it has inaccurately been rated as having the top department in a field in which it does not actually have a department. The nonexistent— but much respected—Princeton Law School is another such example.

The official (or semi-official) rankings of programs provoke complications that may affect which school you think fits you or which ones think you fit them. Start with the most famous ranking system, *US News and World Report*'s yearly graduate program assessment. The magazine's lists have occasioned rejoicing and gnashing of teeth by both faculty (to some extent) and administrators (more so). Basically, the data are generated in two ways. "Experts," such as deans and directors of programs in a field, are asked to rate other programs on a 1 to 5 scale (with 5 being "outstanding"). Then key statistical indicators of the success of a program—such as starting salaries of business school graduates—are created.

Many fields also have ranking scores that they create for themselves. For example, the American Institute of Physics ranks graduate programs using the following criteria:

- total amount of external funding per "full-time equivalent" faculty in the department
- number of peer-reviewed publications per year per capita
- citation index
- enrollment
- graduation rate
- employment of graduates
- ranking by physics departments at other universities

All of these categories produce numbers, but each has qualifications and cannot be interpreted without nuance. Rankings matter to many people—and they should matter to you if you want tenure.

## The Outcome of the Negotiations

The final factor to weigh in whether to take a job is the most elastic one. No unit will change its culture, dean, or P&T document for you, but your deal itself is malleable . . . sometimes. Certainly, you do have the right to negotiate. Doctoral candidates, young faculty, and those with more get-along personalities often experience actual fear of deal-making, or feel it is unseemly. You may be so happy to be wanted, to get any job offer, that the first instinct is to sign whatever contract you are sent.

There are cases where that is the reality: a dean's hiring style may be "take it or leave it." Or the chief administrator may feel that the deal is pretty darn good, the best she can do, and so you should take it. During the writing of this book, while becoming a unit's head administrator for the first time myself, I also made my first solo job offer. It was a reflection of my own experiences and attitudes toward hiring. I loathe bargaining, so I consulted with my higher-ups, studied our budget, and then put together the best possible package I could muster. When I made the offer to our top candidate, I said, "If you can think of something else, fine, but in these particular categories—salary, research funding, and technology—this is the best I can give you." She had made investigations, comparing with new hires in other schools, and agreed. A happy appointment resulted with, I hope, no second-guessing on either party's part about "would've, could've" clauses in negotiation.

Other chairs, deans, and directors hold a much more flexible philosophy, and many job candidates want greater freedom of push-and-pull. An assistant professor in the humanities described a contract letter in which practically every element in it except salary was unspecified. Research funding was vaguely worded as "commensurate with standard." When asked about details, the dean said, "We have to look at our budget [each] year."

Negotiations for a job, thus, are definitely a three-P issue: there are human relations considerations as well as political and personal ones. The dialogue or dance between you and the unit head is not just about numbers or dates but about the first major step in establishing a personal relationship.

**Don't be antagonistic; ask for what is possible.** My first hire was well aware of the range of salary of positions similar to hers at our peer institutions. When my offer met or exceeded all of them, she accepted that she was already touching the ceiling of what she could expect. Relevantly, don't make demands that have no accordance with reality, including the boundaries of the institution and the economy and the basic HR rules of hiring. For example, one humanities finalist asked for double the salary quoted in the job announcement. When the chair of the department stopped laughing, she told him that they could not exceed the maximum advertised amount. If they had double his salary to pay, she explained, they would have opened two positions.

On the other hand, you may very well have a lot of power in this exchange. Some universities do not allow their units to hire second or third choices. The faculty may have been so enthusiastic about you that the unit head would lose face if he or she blew the hire. Ego is also a factor. No matter the temperament of a unit head, they like the idea of bagging the big game, and this is the only example in nature when the game is lucky to be bagged. In one case, a potential new hire was contacted by several of the faculty who had met him on the search visit who joyfully but completely inappropriately told him, "You are our first and only choice. If the dean can't get you, we'll be on the warpath." That was quite helpful information when the candidate entered into negotiations with the sandbagged dean.

Just don't push too hard. If you ask for the moon, a good-natured dean may well give it to you or may indulgently accept that you are young and naïve about what is possible. But don't come off as arrogant, demanding, or peremptory. They can still back away from the deal, saying, "This doesn't seem to be working out." The negotiation process is the ultimate measure of the fit between you and them for both you and them. Always be polite, even when an item is on your categorical list.

No matter how much you sense or know for a fact that they want you, you will have to work with these people for years, and goodwill is always worth more than a few thousand dollars or an upgraded computer.

**Keep in mind the wider politics of your contract.** There is a sad phrase that you will learn later in your career in academia: you have to leave to be loved. The problem of compression in faculty salaries and benefits dogs faculty morale and retention. For many decades, salary levels for new hires rose faster than pay raises for tenured faculty. So understand that although these people voted for you and are probably eager for you to join them, if they learn—and trust me, they will—that you got some astoundingly high salary, the green-eyed monster will not stay in its cave. One young scientist described how, on the first day of his first semester, a senior professor dropped by his office and opened his greeting with, "So, here's the new guy who's making just a few grand less than me!" The young scholar was befuddled. Had he made an enemy before he even started the tenure track?

Then there is the legend at a small liberal arts college of a tough-negotiating new hire getting assigned to a choice parking lot next to the building in which the department was housed. Parking spaces were a mark of stature on campus and, due to the frigid winters, of enormous practical value when navigating icy walks. As this fellow put it, "That parking spot almost cost me tenure. From day one, senior faculty and even staff would bring it up in conversation, sometimes good-naturedly, sometimes with obvious irritation that they were still on a ten-year waiting list to get into the next-door lot. I am convinced that one professor had it in for me from the start because he could look out his office window and see the perk I had that he never got."

So by all means, after having made a realistic appraisal of the possibilities and items you want as well as those you need to take a job, ask for them. But be prepared to take no for an answer, especially if you have only one offer. Moreover, even if you have multiple offers, be ginger in your cross-negotiations.

It is wonderful to be offered a job when on the market for the first time. But calculation is still warranted. Even if the position seems to be a perfect match, ask detailed questions about the deal and the setting. Getting a job is not as permanent as committing to marriage, but neither enterprise should be entered into without knowing as much as you can about the object of your affection—and confirming that your object has commensurably realistic expectations of you.

# Colleagues and Academic Cultures

I began *Promotion and Tenure Confidential* claiming that most newly launched faculty were well trained to do their research, modestly trained to teach, and poorly trained to be *faculty,* considering all the three-P (people, politics, personal) elements affecting survival on the tenure track. This book, thus, has no chapter on how to conduct research. Your mentors in fluvial hydraulics, visual sociology, or Latvian history give you that instruction. Instead, the chapters to come focus on (a) personal qualities you will need to augment, suppress, or develop and (b) academic constituencies that you need to get along with to move past your probationary years with your career and your sanity (and perhaps your health and dignity) intact. The primary audience of import for P&T are your senior colleagues and unit head.

Of course, all the human factors of academic life are interrelated; divisions here are purely for convenience of discussion. Many variables determine your morale and even your physical ability to finish a paper for submission to a journal or to sit through a four-hour faculty meeting without going mad. Your daughter may be sick with the flu; your husband may be disgruntled because you are spending so much time working late in your lab; your students may have zinged you in the course evaluations because you "don't care about them"; and your dissertation advisee may be having a meltdown. Eventually such variables can conspire to deny your tenure.

Equally, you can't ignore one part of the web of activities and issues that comprise your personal/work life and hope to succeed in the others. As considerable research on the topic suggests, if you pay no attention to socialization with your fellow faculty, your pile of publications may come to naught at P&T time.[1] On the other hand, if you focus only on water cooler chatting with the dean but treat your students like dirt, you may be unable to overcome the terrible teaching evaluations you will be hit with.

## One Size Doesn't Fit All . . . But It Can Come Close

An initial issue to address in talking about getting along with colleagues is the generalizability of advice. One of my premises about academic culture is that the *work* of an assistant professor in biology at a major research university may be different than that of an assistant professor of philosophy at a community college or that of an assistant professor of music at a small liberal arts college, but the *human, group, and political* challenges are similar. But what about more physical outliers? Some faculty feel alienated from a system that, despite changes in culture and demography, was designed by and for middle-class, male Anglo-Saxon America.[2]

Compare and contrast stories by two Asian female faculty members, one at an Ivy League university, one at a smaller liberal arts college. The former is now head of a research institute and a well-known and celebrated scholar at the same university where she received tenure. The latter is an assistant professor, denied tenure, with whom I've exchanged correspondence since she contacted me asking for advice. Both faced a similar situation but reacted differently with polar outcomes. Both described how, when they first started the tenure track, most of their colleagues were older white males who from the beginning demonstrated not necessarily hostility, but condescension as well as assumptions of cultural and gender stereotypes. At faculty meetings it was clear that the women were expected to take the notes. Suggestions or even outright requests were made that they cook "delicious" Asian food and serve it at faculty functions. Both thus suffered a range of indignities because they were female and Asian.

My Ivy League friend did not join battle, however. She decided that the wellspring of the prejudicial attitude was ignorance, not malice, and responded accordingly. Coolly and collectedly she told her senior colleagues that she would be happy to share or alternate such duties as taking notes at faculty meetings or occasionally bringing in food but she felt uncomfortable being the exclusive provider of such services. In fact, each time someone treated her differently because of her gender or her race, she countered with gentle persuasion toward better behaviors and attitudes.

Most crucially, *she created a positive professional image of herself* among her colleagues by working hard on her scholarship and being as good a teacher and adviser as she could to students; moreover, she volunteered for more than her share of service work. As she described it, within a few years, although she did not feel like "one of the boys," it was clear that the senior faculty respected her and accepted her in their midst on her own terms. Consistently she was a good colleague to them, and they became good colleagues to her.

My new friend at the small college, however, quite rightfully bridled at the real mistreatment she felt she was receiving and fought back, in protests, complaints, tart exchanges, and grievances filed. Judging from the facts that I've gathered, she was completely justified in all her actions. But the outcome was a long-running feud and permanent enmity between her and practically everyone who would vote on her P&T.

What startled me in our conversation was that she was surprised when she was voted down despite her scholarly achievements. Was she wrong in her response to prejudice? Certainly not morally, ethically, or legally, but we agreed that had she thought through all the permutations and possibilities at the very beginning, the outcome for her might have been different.

Reactions to prejudice need not always be flight or redirection. Rather, those should be among the tools that are considered before you decide on how to counter the slings and arrows of idiots, bigots, or the well-meaning but clueless.

Such cases are legion. I don't offer them to claim that academia is a hotbed of intolerance but that the *cultural* contexts of the academic career are multifaceted. When we advise young faculty to "fit in" to a campus culture, we may, quite sensibly, be suggesting that, for example, if it is the tradition of the professors to dress in more formal attire while teaching, the novice tenure tracker might consider not blazing a bold sartorial trail with a tee shirt and flip-flops. But is it ethical and practical to tell a lesbian to stay in the closet, or a Ceylonese native to not warm up spicy food in the workroom microwave, or a conservative Muslim woman to shake hands with male faculty? That most certainly is *not* my point; rather, I want all young professionals in higher education to be aware that they often have choices about how to react to any perceived provocation.

## After the Hiring Honeymoon

The first year of a job can keep you giddy with joy or filled with tension—or both. You get a rush from being called "professor"; you also find out how hard the tenure-track life can be. But the transition from student to tenure tracker can be hung up on many issues, most prominently the "honeymoon" effect.[3] What follows is a version of an e-mail I wanted—but never felt bold enough—to send a young woman who joined a school where I taught. My intention was to ease her down from her honeymoon high and disappointment after her first year on the job.

*To:* Alice Youngstar, Ph.D., assistant professor, Flagship State University.

*Dear Alice:* You were a very successful Ph.D. student. You got your first tenure-track position at a top research university—ours! The department wooed you for months. The dean made you feel like you were going to be the favored daughter of the program. She checked on you constantly. "Anything we can do to help in any way?" seemed to be her signature refrain.

Indeed, from the time the hiring committee first interviewed you until the day you moved into your office, you felt every bit like this was a match made in ivory-towered heaven. Now, nearing the end of your first year on the faculty, you radiate bewilderment and frustration. You tell me our dean is, by the standards of the hiring honeymoon, inattentive. The e-mail you send to her gets a reply, but not immediately like it did before. During the honeymoon, the answer to your every request was, "I'm sure we can work that out." Now it's, "The budget is tight; we'll have to see." Before, when you called on the phone, her assistant put you right through. Now you are told, "She can squeeze you in in two weeks." When you meet the dean in the hallway, she seems guarded. You just received your first-year evaluation, and it is full of nitpicks. Where once your CV seemed gilded, now there are question marks.

What's wrong? you ask me. Why am I being treated so badly?

Well, I know you, and I know the dean, and I think it's all going to turn out just fine. What's happened to you is natural and normal, and there's no reason to be despondent or to panic. In fact, as you move past this time of unease, you'll grow stronger and be a better teacher, scholar, and colleague for it.

First, understand that judging daily faculty life by the standards of the hiring honeymoon is bound to result in melancholy. All analogies fail if stretched too far, but consider, in parallel, the high failure rate of new marriages. Surely a major problem with marriage is that our culture sets up an ideal model in which newlyweds feel that unless they are levitating with hypnotic affection twenty-four hours a day, somehow the love is gone.

Of course you need love. But you also need horse sense, humor, and patience once kids and car payments start crowding out barefoot walks on moonlit beaches. The high of the honeymoon was great, while it lasted. In academe, as in married life, mastering the workaday routine is the key to long-term success.

For that reason, your dean would fail you if she remained your indulgent aunt for the posthiring era. This is a tough profession; you will face many challenges. The longer someone holds your hand, the longer it will take you to develop the survival skills necessary for independent creativity and production.

The dean can't teach your classes for you, write your research papers, or design your grant proposals. She's not going to coddle you; that's not her job, and you would suffer if she did. She is responsible for thirty-one full- and part-time faculty members, ten staff members, and about 1,000 undergraduate and graduate students. She must answer to several ranks of university and system administrators, and innumerable parents, alumni, and donors. Every one of those people feels his or her needs deserve special attention.

I wager she gets about twenty e-mails a day demanding or whining about something. Some are serious: "Professor X is making advances on me." Some are trivial: "Shall we order orange or yellow sticky notes?" Now, when she sees *your* name on an e-mail, do you want her neurons to snap, "Oh no, not Dr. Crybaby again!"? Maybe she's withdrawn in the hallway because she's anticipating your latest list of complaints. The perpetually squeaky wheel eventually gets ignored or replaced. Or maybe she just had a long, bad day—administrators have them, too, you know.

Try this instead: don't bother your dean with any problem that you can solve for yourself. Don't vent to her: she's not the therapist-in-chief. Save direct appeals for the tough issues. And then walk in with a realistic plan for a solution. Let your name on an e-mail announce something serious and proactive. Be a solver, not a sobber.

Now let's look at the details of the tepid evaluation of your first year.

The research agenda that you filed at the start of the year was too ambitious; the results were comparatively thin. Ah, you respond, I'm a research professor. Shouldn't I reach for the stars? Yes, but studying is not research. It's studying, which is but the necessary prelude to the publication of research.

Another analogy here may be useful. Who were the first people to climb Mount Everest? It may not have been those you think. Two British climbers disappeared while attempting a final ascent on the summit in 1924. No one knows whether they died trying to climb to the top or on the way down afterward. Sir Edmund Hillary, credited officially as one of the first two men to conquer Everest (in 1953), responded to the mystery by noting, "Climbing a mountain means getting to the top and then getting down again."

That's true of research as well. Too many junior faculty members talk about "research" as if the slog (or even the buying of equipment) is the end-all. It is only part of the whole; publication is what counts, and if you just climb up without coming down, you have failed.

The above is not careerist and anti-intellectual; research is something that can be evaluated by your peers—by the world. Better to promise less and complete what you promise. Get a reputation as a doer, not a dreamer.

And let's look at some of the other issues. You tell me, "They hired me for my research potential, but they have me doing service work." How much service work? Trust me, it's not that much compared to the service load that tenured professors carry. And, truly, did not your mood of "I'm a young star so why am I doing this boring stuff?" slow the pace and lessen the quality of your bureaucratic duties? I suspect that's what irritated our dean and the P&T committee. Writing a report on "Improving Peer Student Mentoring in Second-Session Lab Courses" may seem dull to you, but it should be executed with the same level of excellence you would employ to write a research paper. We need such reports, and we want them to come from a faculty member we can trust to do *our* (as in your and the department's) work, not just *her* work, well.

Yes, you will be a star, but you will also have to peel potatoes like the rest of humankind. Accept your new role, and year two will be much improved.

## Managing Up

As my fictive letter implied, there comes a time when every assistant professor, if he or she is to survive in academe, must learn how to "manage up"—to negotiate the intricacies of a relationship with a dean, director, chair, or department head.

Generally, having a bad boss in academia is not as bad as having a bad boss in the private sector. Even if your chair reminds you of Emperor Palpatine in *Star Wars,* it need not be deleterious to your career or even your mental health. As discussed in the previous chapter, people rotate out of chair positions, they step down, and they move on. So if you hold out, maybe a new chair will come along who provides kindly and inspiring leadership. Moreover, unless the chair is truly out to get you for some reason, your P&T won't be just a matter of pleasing him or her but an entire committee of senior faculty; you may find powerful champions and defenders among the latter. And, of course, you can always look for a job elsewhere.

But if you are dealing with rational human behavior among reasonable folk, here are some things you need to know as you learn how to manage your relationship with your bosses.

**Realize that it's not all about you.** You work at an institution with many layers of managers who have their own objectives. Luckily, your interests often coincide with theirs. If you publish enough, teach competently, and stay out of trouble, you and they both look good. But it is vital to be aware of the benchmarks that are particularly attractive to the leadership of your institution. Each unit, for example, has (or should have) formal goals found in a mission statement and a five-year plan. There are also unwritten or implicit aspirations of what the unit wants to be, what they hired you to help achieve.

So, talk to senior professors and your department head about ways in which you can contribute to both. That you would do so in the first place will be noteworthy: most of a department head's meetings with junior faculty members include the latter asking for something. One dean described an assistant professor who began every exchange—no matter the occasion or subject—with "I want." Occasionally, to paraphrase President Kennedy, you need to ask what you can do for your department.

**Pick your whines.** Gaining a reputation as a malcontent will not enhance your career. You may take legitimate grievances to the boss, such as a leaking office roof, a lazy teaching assistant, or a need for more lab money. But it is all too easy, when you perceive you are the suffering party, to get tunnel vision about the relative importance of such problems and to have amnesia about the frequency with which you raise them. Remember that they hired you, in part, because they thought you showed promise to be mature and responsible; you need to show how that promise is being fulfilled by your words and deeds on the tenure track.

One tip on maintaining a macroperspective is to keep a diary of your interactions with authority figures. How many times have you made requests, and for how much? Were they issues that were truly "dean worthy," or could you have handled the problems yourself?

The tone and style of your complaints matter as much as their frequency. Do you present your petitions as reasonable queries or as petulant demands? A simple rule: Never approach a boss with a problem without having investigated two or three practical and affordable solutions.

**Don't make threats.** It is often said that power in academe is not as clearly defined as in most other realms. A professor can outrank a provost in some matters; alternately, according to human resources (HR) rules, a staff assistant might be nearly unfireable. It is tempting for a junior faculty member, overly flattered about his or her own achievements, or unwisely imitating the behavior of his superstar Ph.D. adviser, to try to play the power game. But assuming that you have more power than you actually possess will most likely lead to embarrassment and disaster.

It is possible to get what you want by threatening to resign, for example, and some life-or-death issues may warrant such a threat. But that weapon can only be used once and leaves a trace of acrid smoke in the department ever afterward. No matter how valuable a junior faculty member is, people who have a reputation for all-or-nothing antagonism, a tendency toward the dramatic, or a habit of dropping hints about leaving for other employment will eventually compromise their value. In two cases, the bosses said, "Fine. Good luck on the job market." In one of those cases, the unfortunate assistant professor, it turned out, was bluffing and had to plead momentary insanity as an excuse.

**Understand the protocols of precedent.** While writing this book, I became a unit administrator. I now have certain powers that include control over parts of our budget. Almost immediately I found myself in a novel situation, that of being asked for money—for assistants or technology—and for permission, for things such as taking a leave of absence and teaching a particular course. I try to make such decisions fairly and within our university rules and governance practices. But I have learned that one of the most powerful inhibitors to my dispensing goodies and favors is that of precedent. Simply put, what I give one faculty member sets a precedent for others to ask. If I approve exceeding the standard travel funding allotment for one professor, then twenty others, potentially, have the right to ask the same of me—and query why I willingly violated the policy I was charged to monitor.

Most faculty are not selfish, but they do tend to see the virtue of their particular request and not the wider issue of precedent that all administrators learn to weigh in making decisions. Assistant professors will be well regarded by their deans if they at least appreciate the precedent issue. A denial may not be a condemning verdict on a proposal but rather a reflection of the effect it will have on others.

**Don't dodge the grunt work.** Show up for meetings. Answer your e-mail. Attend your office hours. Every profession, every job, entails activities that are unromantic and seemingly lacking in value for the individual. Academia is full of tedious committee assignments, problem-student advising, and reports that few will read. No supervisor should load up junior faculty members with such tasks to the point that they cannot focus on their primary goals of teaching and research.

At the same time, no assistant professor should think that personal gratification—teaching only the courses you like, advising only the students who intrigue you, and doing only the committee work directly related to your research—is possible or politically acceptable. Here again, maturity and responsibility should be your creed, the descriptors that your senior faculty use when describing you.

**Avoid bad blood.** Only after you start a new job do you discover the factional fissures and intradepartmental rivalries. Senior professors may try to involve you in their fights or ask you to take a side. You should state clearly, if asked, "I think while I'm on the tenure track I should just concentrate on my work and not get into a battle with anyone." Only the most boorish and fanatical senior professor will, at that point, keep pushing you to join in his crusade.

Then there is the allure of joining in when others—the tenured class—are belittling the administrators. It is oh-so-tempting to take part in the fun, and oh-so-fatal when a supervisor later hears about your witticism made at her expense. It seems obvious but apparently needs to be said: don't publicly deride anyone, but especially don't deride someone who is going to vote on your future or decide your salary. Remember also, when you trash-talk someone, other people might be laughing but they're also thinking, "What does he say about me when I'm not in the room?"

**Remember that dissent is fine . . . sometimes; discord is not.** One assistant professor argued about almost every subject the department faced. "In some cases he was right," the chair said. "But in all cases, he was irksome and alarming. Even people who agreed with him on a point were thinking, 'Whoa, do we really want this guy around for 30 years?'" Obviously, you need to strike a balance here. There is no reason to become a toady, but your "nays" should never take on the appearance of personal attack or vendetta. Some simple "thou shalt nots" apply.

- Don't raise your voice or lose your temper—ever!
- Don't challenge some ingrained unit tradition that has strong senior champions (until after tenure).
- Don't fight over anything unless you have researched it well enough to make sure the facts are on your side.
- Don't take up any struggle without vetting your position with trusted mentors who can give you some history and some perspective.
- Don't adopt—no matter how in-the-right you are—a tone of righteousness or categoricalness.
- Don't try to score points on the cleverness scale by embarrassing your unit head in public.

Remember that as a junior, a probationary faculty member, you can lose the war (P&T) even if you win a victory over a minor issue of curriculum or procedure. (I will elaborate more on this vital issue in the section on picking battles.)

**Learn to acknowledge defeat.** Faculties vote, deans make decisions, and you will be judged not only by the frequency and tone of your opposition but by how graciously you accept that it did not carry the day. Every good employer appreciates an employee with this philosophy: "I'll tell you what I think even if you don't want to hear it, but at the end of the day, if we go in another direction, I'll do my best to make it happen." Following these guidelines will not convert you into a vocational mouse, nor will they have you groveling before your "betters." Academia is indeed all about mutual respect. But for the newly minted Ph.D., respect must be earned slowly, over time, by your efforts in research, teaching, and service. Integral to success in all three categories is your attitude in managing your manager.

## Do You Really Not Have the Time?

A student sits in your office lamenting his low grade on a midterm exam. He tells you he fared poorly because he did not have enough time to study. Curious, you ask him to catalog how he spends his days and nights during an average week. It turns out that partying, concerts, and playing video games rank high, so that "not enough time *to* study" really meant "not enough time *spent* studying."

We all see students who are woefully unskilled at organizing their calendars, who start term papers at the last minute, or who assume that late bar-hopping on a weeknight will not affect their concentration during an exam the next morning. In addition, the multimedia aspect of their actual study time—plugged in, linked up, online—is hardly conducive to the retention of information. People have a finite attention span, and "multitasking" just means reducing the quality of our focus on individual tasks.[4] The irony is that many of us faculty members could use some time-management advice as well.

Few tenure trackers fail because of the distractions of fraternity keggers or playing too much *Halo 3*. But we all hear faculty members say they don't have enough time to do their research, prepare for a class, attend meetings, or even to live their lives.[5] In many cases, it may be true—to a point. But it's also true that we can all afford to step back and assess whether we are managing our time efficiently.

To get your work life under control, you must recognize that there is a problem. In 2006, a management-research company named Basex conducted a study of workplace productivity among 1,000 white-collar employees and found that a whopping 2.1 hours of their day were consumed by interruptions.[6] Worse, workers reported that when they stopped to check their e-mail messages it took almost half an hour to return to their real work.

There is hope. The management of time and the reduction of disruptive distractions—as opposed to the positive kind reviewed in the next chapter—in academia are not impossible goals.[7] And having a clear "sense of purpose" such as "must get tenure!" confirms the need to arrange our time well.[8]

The first step is to stake out your preferred work environment. All the productive academics have a "Walden," a place they can go, as Thoreau put it, to "transact some private business with the fewest obstacles." Perhaps for you it's a literal cabin in the woods or a carrel in the library. Temperament matters in the choice. Some people can't do creative work unless they have absolute peace and quiet, the "sterile cockpit" recommended in flight safety and the operating room to maximize attention and avoid possible disturbances.[9] Others can write up research or grade papers in Grand Central Station.

Whatever your favored venue, carve out time to concentrate there. As an assistant professor, parts of your job—teaching duties, meetings, and office hours—may call for your presence at the office. But on many if not most research campuses, faculty members are not expected to sit at a desk chair with an open door from 8 a.m. to 5 p.m. Devote a set time each week to doing your creative work without checking e-mail or answering the phone. Keep that creative period sacred; surrender it only for a true crisis.

Frame of mind also matters. You can accomplish a lot in ten hours a week of determined effort as opposed to forty hours of scattershot, interrupted work. Simply shutting out physical distractions is not enough: harking back to the suggestion made earlier about the mind-spirit evenness that you needed to finish a dissertation, you must summon some spiritual focus here as well—a sort of "Zen and the Art of Research." Perhaps your creative-work time begins with yoga, meditation, t'ai chi, prayer, or a much-needed nap. Any ritual that cleanses the mind of unproductive intrusions will do.

Think about how to avoid pop-up distractions or interruptions.[10] One of the reasons academics postpone starting or completing big projects is because it is so easy to be diverted by minutiae. A friend of mine used to tell people, "If I don't get tenure it will be because of e-mail." He was only half joking. You can check e-mail once a day or less without the world ending; there's no need to scan your BlackBerry or iPhone at any other time. Above all, train your students not to expect instant replies: put in your syllabus that you will check your e-mail at a set time each day and they can expect replies after that. Perhaps it's antediluvian advice, but I fail to see why *any* assistant professor needs to exchange text messages or instant messaging with students. You might add, though, to use the phone in the case of emergencies—but be sure to define "emergency." As will be discussed more in the chapter on student relations, the trick is to reduce your distractions while still convincing the students that you care about them.

## Planning Projects

Once you have some hope for getting work done, you need to plan for the work, in the same sense as an artist sketching out a painting and an architect drawing up blueprints. Begin with the big picture: consider what you want to complete in teaching, research, and service, and calculate the probable time needed to finish the projects for, say, three years ahead. Then create a time/project chart (several software programs for project planning are on the market). Your mentors can help you make a reasonable assessment of how much time particular projects are likely to take. Make your chart as snazzy and professional as possible, and place it prominently in your office. Review once a week.

Sounds like the ways of a sales representative, not an intellectual? Yes, but a physical chart is a visible reminder of your priorities: to avoid missing a deadline, it helps to see it looming. The chart demonstrates that your time is limited—to add a new project, you have to subtract one. And it shows people (like, say, senior professors or your chair) that you are organized. Trust me, even if they tease you, they will be impressed.

Of course, if you don't actually use the chart, they won't be impressed for long. You have to convince yourself and the people around you, from your family to your dean, that the chart reflects a conceptualization that you are trying to bring to life. For example, a spouse or partner who is not an academic might like to see the tangible requirements of your work on journal articles and understand the penalties of failure. Alternatively, the chart might help persuade your chair to support your budget requests.

I got my family on my side when, while working on a book, I put my young children in charge of monitoring my progress. They gave me a little gold star when I finished a chapter on time. They were also much more understanding when Daddy had to close his home-office door in order to focus on work.

Perhaps charts and gold stars are too cheesy for you, but the essence of time management should not be. Plan ahead. Project how much time and resources you will need to finish. Learn to distinguish between tasks that deserve immediate attention and those that can be forgotten. Inculcate a personal philosophy that allows you to focus on the project at hand to the exclusion of all other distractions.

## How to Say No (and Get Away With It)

Deciding to focus on the vital projects, managing your time, and reducing distractions are all engines of success on the P&T track. The great brakeman, however, is that assistant professors have less control over their own time than the tenured class. Consider these common scenarios.

*Case 1:* You are sitting in your office, poring over some data from your most recent experiment. If you can just get a few more hours of work in today, you might be able to submit a paper for a national conference before the deadline.

Suddenly, a senior professor knocks. It is Von Slug, head of the department's tenure committee. "I have some great news," he states cheerily. He has started a major new research project, and he wants you to be his partner and coauthor. You freeze: A big start-up project would throw off your research agenda and publishing schedule. You are also aware of Von Slug's reputation—"coauthor" means "you do the work and I'll sign my name to the publications." But how can you say no to a man who, at least in part, oversees your P&T destiny?

*Case 2:* Albert, your first doctoral student, keeps changing his topic, taking up more and more of your time, and falling behind in the work he is doing (badly) as your assistant. As the semester ends, you delicately bring up the possibility of his finding a more compatible adviser and supervisor. He is astonished. You are the "only one in the university who really cares." Three other senior professors have given up on him (which is true). Should you muddle along in the relationship for months, perhaps years, knowing in your heart that he will never finish and all your time and effort will be wasted?

Both cases convey the same point: the single most important people, political, and personal skill a junior faculty member can develop is the ability to say no and stand by it, after gauging whether refusing a request is or is not an option. An inability to say no is a widespread problem in many professions, judging by dozens of self-help books on the subject. But academia presents some special circumstances that make the quandary particularly tricky.

On the pragmatic side, there are people in our work lives who hold what might be termed "ambiguous power" over us. A senior professor asks a favor: he does not have the power to fire you, lower your salary, or get you transferred to the north Alaskan office as would a senior executive in the corporate world. But maybe that professor will nurse a grudge come time to vote on your tenure case.

Then there is the psychological dimension of saying no. That, too, is a familiar issue outside academia; a number of self-help texts promise to instruct readers how to say no without guilt. But declining a request is especially problematic for young professors who, after all, become teachers because they like to help others. We academics are built, by inclination and training, to be "yes" people.

Fear and guilt are real feelings not easily dismissed. But there are strategies that will lessen the odds that your refusal will be taken as a personal affront and that will allow you to satisfy your own conscience.

Let's return to case 1: how should you deflect Professor Von Slug in his quest to sign you up as his new research partner? Your initial reply should sound something like this: "That's interesting and promising. I'm honored you would ask me. Let me look over the details." In other words, be polite but delay an answer until you can take the following steps:

- Develop an accurate assessment of the size and scope of the proposed project.
- Consult your unit head and trusted mentors about the proposal.
- Weigh how working on the project will affect all of your other labors, not to mention your personal life.
- Assess the tangible benefits of success in the project. Would it lead to publications that will boost your tenure case?

If you decide not to commit to the project, diplomatically say, "This sounds great, but I am already in the middle of these other tasks, and if I took on your project, I'm afraid I would not have time to do it justice." Here is one payoff for making that time management chart I described above look both snappy and serious instead of mere scrawls on the back of an envelope. You have evidence to show Von Slug of how busy and committed you already are.

Sure, he may feel spurned and react badly. But if you are sincere, pleasant, and forthright—giving him an early answer, without ducking—he may leave impressed by your professionalism and organizational skills. On some level, the Von Slugs of academe understand that learning to say no helped them achieve their own career goals. Perhaps he may even decide that, because you are so busy, you probably would not be the best mule to carry his pack.

The key to saying no with few repercussions, thus, is to avoid rejecting a proposal out of hand, without due thought. Show that you've considered the offer seriously. Describe your logic. Explain your reasons. Tone and body language matter: we all know people who, as the saying goes, can make enemies by the way they say yes and friends by the way they say no.

Denying a request can also be justified by simple fairness. Say an undergraduate begs you to change her low grade. She will lose her scholarship, upset her sick grandmother, or fail to achieve her dream of getting her B.A. in seven years unless you relent and let her do some quick extra credit work to bring up her grade. That is a case where you could use institutional policies—such as those stipulating that points in a course must be available to all students, not just one—to make clear that your no means no.

Another technique for saying no to something you don't want to do or can't do is to lay out the alternatives to a "yes." Perhaps your department chair has asked you to take on a new service project that you fear would interfere unduly with your other work. Turn the question around; show your chair what you are working on—that chart again!—and say sincerely, "I would love your advice on what I should give up in order to do this new thing."

Woe to the assistant professor who refuses all service work. But when you do commit to something, as stated in the chapter on doctoral studies, follow the advice of Ecclesiastes to "do it with thy might." In fact, that's often the best argument for declining further requests: because saying yes would jeopardize your proven success elsewhere. Maybe it will be a simple matter of horse-trading one service project for another. Perhaps your chair will insist; but I suspect that, in the future, the message will register that when you say you are busy, you mean it.

Which brings us back to Albert, the troubled graduate student. In some ways, his case is thornier than others. Say no to Von Slug, and the only one who gets hurt is you (but the wound is less grievous than if you had committed to his project). But wouldn't saying no to Albert tear asunder some sacred code of selflessly aiding students? A vital consideration is whether your efforts can *really* help Albert. I quote a veteran professor: "You can't drag them across the finish line." So, objectively, even if you gave Albert your maximum effort, maybe you would just be delaying the inevitable and prolonging the pain for both of you.

Saying no in such instances is difficult, and the consequences are uncertain. But to survive the tenure track, your first loyalty has to be to your career. This advice may sound Machiavellian, but at the end of the day, you provide no service to anyone if you fail to get tenure. Your highest duty is to become a productive member of the faculty. Being a doormat for all and sundry requests will sabotage that goal. Don't become like the proverbial pastor who spends so much time helping his flock that his own family falls apart.

## Problem People

*Promotion and Tenure Confidential* is about the three Ps, and a core concern of people, politics, and personal issues are those of our peers on the faculty who are problems—to students, staff, everybody, or maybe just to you. The definition of a "problem person" is as infinite as the human condition—which is one reason I don't have separate sections on each kind of dysfunction of *Homo sapiens*. Certainly, people with social or psychological eccentricities that would get them fired in a normal workplace without the protection of tenure, or in a work environment where they would be heavily supervised or observed, can survive and thrive in academia, or at least they have in the past. But almost always, when you are on the tenure track and you encounter a problem person, unless you plan to quit and get another job, or file an HR grievance or start a fight, you have to assess the situation and ask two basic questions that cut across all the kinds of difficulties human beings can have with each other.

**Is this person's problem chaotic or predictable?** A social science professor looking back at the first part of his career, which included a job switch while he was still on the tenure track, described the polar contrast between the two deans she had worked under. One was a classic dictator: insecure, hair-trigger temper, vindictive, micromanaging, but completely an Old Faithful of dependability in his wants, needs, and opinions. If she stayed on his good side, everything was fine. And after a semester, she had picked up exactly how to stay on his good side. In short, the tenure tracker found that it was always her own choice whether to anger or irritate her boss, and on almost every issue her own work was not really affected. She decided the cost of mollifying him was slight and also felt confident that she knew how to do so.

In contrast, her second dean was low-key, but he was also wildly unpredictable. He would switch positions, or become cryptic, or just seem to hold contradictory views. She never knew where she stood with him. The irony was that the young scholar had left her first position in part to escape the tyrant only to find that she preferred dependable authoritarianism over chaotic anarchy.

Sometimes we have to make the same decisions about our colleagues. Gruff, irascible curmudgeons can end up not being too difficult to deal with if you figure out what their hot buttons are and, if they're not particularly important to you, don't press those. Passive-aggressive "friends" might be more dangerous to deal with because you never know what will get them enthused or enraged.

**Is this person truly undermining or truly supportive?** At a faculty reception once, I found myself seated at a table of unhappy assistant professors, all of whom were either new to the tenure track or had been on it for just a few years. The encounter brought to mind a *Far Side* cartoon in which a group of circus clowns gathers at a therapy session and one asks, "Gee, am I the only one here who is laughing on the outside and the inside?"

While we can all feel buoyed up by a cheerleader in our lives, sometimes uncritical and undiscerning support is actually dysfunctional. Assistant professors like the ones described above might fall into this category. A young colleague once described biweekly luncheons with his tenure-track cohort. They jokingly called it "the W&B hour" (whine and bitch), and indeed, from his description, no event seemed to escape their catalogue of the woes and horrors they individually suffered. There was an echo chamber effect: one complaint would bounce off another and magnify the intensity of each. I advised my friend to drop out of the group for a month or two; he did, and found that both his mood and his productivity improved.

I don't advocate shunning fellow assistant professors, and we all need shoulders to cry on and people to tell us that we're worthwhile. But the tenure-track years are stressful enough without embracing a circle of disparagers who incite a spiral of despair. You do need assistant professor pals who support you emotionally, who commiserate with your suffering. However, you also need those who are willing to objectively appraise your reports of persecution or ask gently whether the problem person in some conflict you have, perhaps with a student, staff member, tenured professor, or administrator, is *you*. The young scholar formed a splinter group with one of the other tenure trackers who also had begun to doubt whether W&B was of any assistance to

P&T. The two met once a month to toast to and chuckle at their problems, and to discuss and critically review possible, practical solutions. A variation on the question of supportiveness is also provoked by peers who seem to enjoy being your foxhole buddy. Foxhole buddies come in many guises. One, an assistant professor in the arts recounted, was a senior faculty member who, spotting a tenure tracker's door open, would saunter in and spin doomsday scenarios. He would allege, "In confidence, this professor doesn't like you. That graduate student said you are a bad teacher. The chair didn't think much of your research." And so on. After a while, the tenure tracker discerned that it was all lies, exaggerations, and unfounded conspiracy theories. The dysfunctional gray fox enjoyed stirring up trouble and setting up relationships with junior faculty so that they felt he was their one true protector ("it's you and me against the bad guys, kid"). The solution was to listen politely, nod gravely, and then get back to work.

## Secrets and Gossiping

That foxhole buddies cause so much damage is testament to the fact that no one trains academics to deal with the etiquette and ethics of campus secrets or the challenges that arise when you tell or hear one. Yet this is a facet of the P&T process—another one that does not fall neatly into the categories of teaching, research, or service.

Newcomers to the tenure track must learn their institution's rules for safeguarding all sorts of information, not just gossip. Thanks to the Family Educational Rights and Privacy Act (FERPA), there are rules about what you can and can't say about students. Other policies govern aspects of academia like when to circulate news of a job opening in your department. Even information that is "secret" in one setting is not in another: outside letters of review for P&T are kept confidential at many institutions but can be disclosed in lawsuits. If all that seems complicated, the rules for dealing with private confidences—including dirt, rumors, and innuendo—are even more so.

Let's start by considering a lesson learned by historians and spies: secret information is not necessarily more accurate than common knowledge. We all have been dupes, willing and otherwise, of some self-described insider who informs us with great portent, "I know what really happened." Later we may discover multiple alternative realities of the "true story." There is a romantic aura to tidbits transmitted in a whispered confidence rather than via a public document on a university Web site, but secrets rarely get more accurate with repetition. Disinformation is a common strategy, whether among nations in armed conflict or professors indulging their preexisting annoyance with each other.

The obvious moral for academics, living in our professional "small towns" and dependent on the goodwill of our neighbors, is one of discretion. Don't believe everything you are told, whether it is printed on official university letterhead or muttered behind a ginkgo tree in the quad. Certainly, don't act on gossip-borne information unless you verify that it's true or if it is the kind of allegation that your university rules dictate must be reported immediately.

Realize, also, that we all possess a finite amount of reputational credibility. Long ago, as a first-year faculty member, I met a fellow I will call Professor Gloom. He regularly made dire predictions based on what he claimed was insider knowledge about the future of the university. At first, he frightened me enough to make me wonder if I had made a mistake in accepting the job. Gradually, I caught on that his "sky is falling" prognostications (a) never panned out and (b) were projections of his own unhappiness.

My reaction then was to politely pretend to listen to him while actually daydreaming about my pet hamster. I found myself automatically, and perhaps unfairly, discounting his opinions on *all* subjects, including ones he actually knew a great deal about. The point is that, among the many reasons why you should not share a secret in academia, the most important is that you might be wrong about the facts.

For new faculty members, moreover, knowing how and when to share a secret or keep one is particularly perplexing. In this era of cellphone videos, YouTube, and blogging, it seems like people are exposing information about themselves and others at an unprecedented rate.

Almost everyone finds privileged information enthralling, particularly if you are new to a profession and if the gossip involves someone who has nominal authority over you. Sharing a secret about your supervisor makes you feel you have some degree of control over the more powerful, but the feeling is ephemeral. In academia, secrets flow uphill faster than they trickle downhill. A department head or director is much more apt to be tipped off to a rumor that is becoming commonly known than, say, the newest tenure-track hire. And the higher up you are in our profession, the more probable the secrets you tell will be kept quiet, out of loyalty as well as prudence. Betraying the confidence of a provost is much more likely to have negative consequences for the tattletale than passing on the secret of a post-doc.

Even so, there is no guarantee that any secret will remain unrevealed. I once got into a dispute with another professor during which he let slip some information about me—incorrect, as it turns out—that he had heard from a colleague of ours. I had to ask him, "Did she mean for you to tell me this?" He shrugged and said something to the effect that it was hard to keep a secret in the heat of battle.

Indeed, when personal relations clash with institutional responsibilities, things gets complicated, especially if you are lower on the academic food chain. As discussed in the previous chapter, on-the-job job hunting is a pregnant area for such contretemps. A professor cited the predicament of a newly hired young colleague who had confided that he hated his job, disliked living in the area, was applying for positions elsewhere, wanted a letter of reference, and would like his exit activities "kept quiet." But the senior professor was part of the department's technology committee, so when a request came in from the young scholar for a great deal of new equipment, the senior member recommended it be denied.

A variation of that story comes from another professor. A young colleague told her that his wife "would never be happy in this town, and we just want to get out," but, of course, "this is just between you and me." The problem: Shortly afterward, he asked for a large raise to match an outside job offer. The senior professor decided to inform the dean about what the young man had said, because it was clear that an extra payout would only delay an inevitable exit.

Information you share in confidence has a way of getting out. While there is no one-size-fits-all approach to handling academic secrets, some caveats are worth keeping in mind.

First, the best way to avoid the complications of gossip is not to trade in it. Before you confide personal information to a colleague, ask yourself: Do I really need to reveal this? Would I be happy if that confidence were transmitted to, well, the world? Who is hurt, and who is helped? What is the price of this "private" matter being relayed to someone else, especially to a supervisor?

Alternately, when you're about to be on the receiving end of a secret, practice saying, "I think I know what you are going to tell me, and it's really none of my business. Gotta run." The amount of time and grief that phrase can save you is inestimable.

Of crucial, perhaps job-saving, importance is the understanding that there are some secrets you cannot keep, legally or because of the ethics and HR policy rules of your university. An assistant professor described how a graduate student came to her claiming that a professor had made some inappropriate physical advances. The assistant professor tried to take up the matter herself, hoping to avoid trouble. She had several fruitless conversations with both parties, which only entangled her in the dispute. The graduate student subsequently filed an official complaint. The university reprimanded the assistant professor for failing to report immediately, as HR policy unequivocally required, that a possible case of sexual harassment had taken place. Provosts and deans have toppled because they have ignored laws and rules like this one; you have no volition in such matters.

### Pick Your Battles . . . But How?

The Roman philosopher Seneca argued, "A contest with one's equal is hazardous, with a superior mad, with an inferior degrading."[11] He had firsthand knowledge about the second clause: he was banished by one emperor and killed by another. Likewise, the advice that tenure-track academics seek and receive about P&T can vary a great deal, depending on whether you teach at a community college or a research university, or study fruit fly genetics or constructions of identity in Racine's plays. But there are certain consistent counsels that apply to all disciplines, institutions, and life situations. One that I have both gotten and offered seems self-evidently universal: *pick your battles.* There is considerable confusion, however, about how, when, and why to put the advice into practice.

Just as for a military general in the field, many "battles" that confront us are obfuscated by the fog of war. Without the vantage point of hindsight, we do not necessarily know (a) whether a battle is imminent; (b) what the short-term and long-term costs or benefits of fighting the battle are; (c) what the likely outcomes of the battle are; and (d) what alternatives to combat are available.

Let me give three examples.

1. *The review from hell.* You get back the reviews to a journal article submission. One is positive, with moderate suggestions for changes before acceptance. The second trashes your theory, method, even choice of a topic. The journal editor, in his letter, states that he must reject the paper based on such a strongly negative review. But you feel the evisceration was not only cruel but factually wrong: the negative reviewer made consistent mistakes in the description of your points and data.

Do you move on, taking the article to another journal, or do you write back to the editor fully detailing and documenting the iniquity of your persecutor and demand that the review itself be negated?

2. *The dissertation defense offense.* You are the adviser for a doctoral candidate who is defending her dissertation. One of the members of the committee has been consistently tardy in reading previous drafts and uncommunicative in responding with any usable commentary. The morning of the defense, you call him at home; he assures you that he is basically happy with the current draft of the dissertation (which has been on his desk for months) and will not make any trouble. Suddenly, however, in the midst of the defense, he raises some radically new ideas for further work that, if your advisee responded to them, would alter the entire project, delaying her graduation by a year or more.

Do you accept the "advice" or do you protest, bringing up the professor's earlier assurance of accord, and try to squash his interjections in front of the entire committee, including the representative of the graduate school, the witnessing student audience, and your advisee?

3. *The unfair annual evaluation.* You are a new, untenured faculty member and have just received your letter of yearly evaluation from your

chair. It recounts in laudatory language your many accomplishments. Then you note that your merit pay increase is well below the campus and departmental average. A first tentative and polite note to the chair gets a frosty response and the rejoinder that "we followed our formula."

Do you ask for more specifics, and then if the chair will not give you satisfaction, appeal to the dean of the college and beyond?

In each case, battle is an option, but so is silence and retreat, or something in between. Making a decision about whether this is a battle worth fighting should not, however, be left to instinct alone. Before lowering your lance for a charge, take into account the following.

**Who is in the right?** It is a natural human tendency to see ourselves in the best possible light and to see others—especially if they oppose or attack us—in the worst. But a heroic self-image can be self-destructive if it leads you to career off into a melee when the facts are not so clearcut. It's always useful to step back and at least think about the case for the opposition. You may not change your mind, but at least you will have some idea of your antagonist's possible motivations.

In case 1, there is some ambiguity: after all, a reviewer has the right to review, and you can understand that a journal editor is reluctant to allow authors, in effect, to expunge reviews that they don't like. In case 2, maybe the flaws that the committee member uncovered do exist. But the holder of the ethical right is pretty clear: students should not be ambushed at dissertation defenses. In case 3, you don't have enough information to know who is right: maybe you did not perform well according to the mysterious formula, although, if so, the shortcomings should have been enumerated in the letter.

**What is the optimum timing of your response?** An assistant professor was insulted by a comment made by a fellow faculty member at a meeting and simmered and stewed about it for months. Finally, at another meeting on a wholly different topic, he lashed out at his nemesis. The problem was that everybody else had forgotten the initial provocation, so the "victim" came off looking like an aggressor without a cause. Your response must make temporal sense, which depends on the nature and venue of the provocation.

In scenario 1 above, you have time, months even, to respond to the review. That will allow you to muster a good case, documenting in detail the negative reviewer's mistakes. In scenario 2, you have a much shorter window: you can't delay a response until after the defense. In scenario 3, you have at least a few weeks to get more information from other (trusted) faculty about the evaluation formula.

**How ready are you for battle?** You don't have to be an acolyte of Sun Tzu to know that when you go into combat you should be pretty sure you have the necessary resources to win. In case 1, no journal editor will change his mind just based on protests: you will need to mount a detailed argument. In case 2, documentation is tricky because it's a he-said/he-said situation: the uppity committee member can always claim you misunderstood him in the phone call. In case 3, you have your original hiring contract, which should contain some language about the criteria you will be evaluated on, and the department *should* have an explanation of its formula.

**Who will be your allies in a battle?** Allies, in war and in office politics, can sometimes be a burden, drawing us into unwanted battles. Napoleon once said that he would rather fight allies than be one; of course, he was defeated by a coalition of enemies. Likewise, useful, powerful allies can help if you choose to fight a battle, but in academia people are reluctant to leap into what they perceive as a personal fight in which they have no stake.

In case 1, you are definitely alone: you would look childish if you brought other parties into your appeal. The only exception is if you were a protégé of a powerful member of the journal's editorial board, and even then you should ask only for advice, not an intervention. In case 2, did you share your worries about the dissenting member's slacker behavior beforehand with another committee member? Had the doctoral candidate come to you with concerns earlier? What you hope is that other members of the committee, preferably including a senior, are as outraged as you and, if there is a fight, they will take the lead. In case 3, you are probably alone, unless a number of other faculty are unhappy with the "formula" and start a movement to refine it.

Escalation—to go above the head of the chair—is truly risky because a dean of the college would be loath to overrule a department head on an internal matter. You may find horizontal allies but not vertical ones.

**Are you fully aware of the connections, capabilities, and attitudes of the enemy?** In war or in barroom disputes, it is highly inadvisable to get into a fight unless you know something about your enemy's skills, resources, and level of implacability. In academia, people have their "byline power"—that is, the power that goes with their job title, from provost to assistant professor to graduate assistant. There are, however, interconnections that are not always self-evident, especially to the newbie. A secretary may have long-standing friends in the administration or among the senior professors. A graduate student may be the niece of a powerful alumnus. In theory, the power of an enemy should not stop you from standing up for what is just, but it should affect how you do so.

In all three cases above, the enemies you gain objectively outrank you—hence the need for allies or avoidance of a fight.

**How much time and effort will the battle cost?** A risk-reward equation is useful to warlords and assistant professors alike. In some cases, you will have morality, ethics, the facts, and every other consideration in your favor but decide that fighting a battle is still unwise because it will use up too great a proportion of resources (time, attention, social capital, and sanity). Unfortunately, there are faculty—like the foxhole buddies described earlier—who, apparently bored by research, teaching, or service, enjoy getting into squabbles. You always lose when you engage them.

In case 1, you must anticipate at least several days of careful documentation and letter crafting. The good side is that all of it is focused on your research and thus will probably be of use in future writings. I have found that the act of writing revise-and-resubmit cover letters helps improve my work.

In case 2, the efforts will be short term: a dispute in the room for a few hours, unless it becomes a matter of appeals and counterappeals and complaints to the chair or the dean of the graduate school.

In case 3, the work will be minimal: your CV and teaching portfolio should be all you need, again unless it becomes a mushroomed imbroglio with letters to others. But in cases 2 and 3, the chances for mental strain are high, and subsequent follow-up scuffles are likely.

**What are the possible consequences of a fight?** Many an army has embarked with high hopes of fighting a quick, decisive battle and getting home for Christmas, but the contingencies set off by war are often opaque at its conception. In academia, there are obvious dangers if you fight a battle, but there are unforeseen ones as well. The most important consequence might be the effect on your image: faculty who get into lots of battles, even if every one is justifiable, get known for causing trouble, *and nobody wants to hire or tenure and promote a troublemaker.*

A big red question mark sticks to your CV when you try to find another job. You do not want to earn, albeit unfairly, a reputation as a bad apple.[12] So, have you fought your quota of battles for the year—for your career? Also, some people have more at stake than others. The common wisdom is correct: it is very chancy for probationary professors to get into a fight with anyone, especially senior faculty.

In case 1, the bad review, a battle will probably result in few lasting damages beyond antagonizing a journal editor. The reviewer, if confidentiality is maintained, will not know your name unless she deduced it from clues in the manuscript or sees the essay in print later. The journal editor may end up respecting your due diligence even if it costs him some worry and fuss. And—who knows?—you might win and get published.

In case 2, the dissertation dispute, a short-term victory would result in the student passing. The damages, however, may be limited but long-standing. Get into a verbal brawl with a professor, practically accuse him of unethical behavior, and you will have made an enemy for life.

In case 3, the unfair evaluation, it depends how far you push your chair. If all you ask for is clarification, then the damage should be light. (And the formula may work in your favor next time.) If you start mobilizing faculty alliances and appealing to the dean, you are declaring war. But short-term victory is unlikely: your chair would have to admit that he was wrong about pay increases, which makes him lose face and opens him up to appeals from the whole faculty.

Picking a battle to fight, thus, is not straightforward. The dangers of some situations are self-evident. The real question is whether alternative paths to conflict resolution exist that bypass the battlefield in the first place.

In case 1, for example, tone will matter a great deal in the likely response you get to an appeal. You can document voluminously the facts to the journal editor but remain tactful: "I think there was a misunderstanding in the review . . ." instead of "You really blew it, you goofball." Indeed, in the real-life incident from which this case was drawn, the journal editor agreed to "extend the review" mainly because the author made a strong case with facts and without accusations. The editor sought out an additional reviewer, who gave the article positive marks. Publication ensued, and there were no hard feelings and no battles. Mission accomplished.

In case 2, the assistant professor who headed the committee also solved the problem without a battle. He let everyone have their say, including the difficult committee member. As the commentary and exchanges continued, it was clear that the other committee members all felt that the dissertation was fine and needed only minor revisions. By the end of the meeting, the snarky professor understood he was the sole voice of opposition; he, in turn, felt his position was not worth fighting about. After the candidate left the room, the committee chair went out of his way to be solicitous to the professor. He also suggested that the outlier's advice could be incorporated into a projection for future research in the concluding chapter. Everyone agreed, and everyone went home thinking each had made a contribution. Another Ph.D. was born, and a battle was avoided.

The third case also ended well for the protagonist. He wrote a polite note to the department chair saying, in effect, "I'm new here and eager to be of maximum service to the school. I would just like to review, so that I know for next time, the details of the formula I will be judged by each year." The chair agreed to meet and offered the formula, which was vague and subjective indeed. The young scholar took this as a cue that he was working in a dysfunctional system. He bided his time, focused on productivity, and got a better job elsewhere. (Moreover, his in-program references noted his collegiality and reasonableness.)

In sum, picking the battles to fight means thinking about their meaning within the scheme of your life and your career, not just giving way to passions of the moment or your feeling of victimization. In the world and in academia, sometimes the best way to win a battle is to avoid fighting it at all.

## Presenting Yourself Virtually: Social Media and P&T

As we have seen, "the presentation of self" is a critical aspect of pursuing an academic career. Once upon a time, such concerns would have been limited to how people saw you in person and through your print publications. But now an entirely new world of impressions and self-presentation is available and likely heavily employed by young academics, although not always to their credit.

For example, during the writing of this book, and just before I began a position as head of a unit, I radically changed the way the world sees me—the Facebook world, that is. For years, my profile picture on the immensely popular social Web site had been a coin portrait of the Roman dictator Sulla. The representation was meant to be a joke because he was proverbially malicious, ruthless, and careerist, and I hoped people didn't see me that way. More than once, however, students (and some colleagues) interpreted my choice of picture as a statement of principle and personality. Their knowledge of Sulla, drawn from Wikipedia or elsewhere, led them to the conclusion that, although he may have been a great general and a hugely successful politician, you probably would not want to take his class on media ethics, and you might not feel comfortable with him in charge of your yearly evaluation.

So now my nonthreatening profile picture is of one of our family's cats.

The vast new world of online social-interactive media—Facebook, MySpace, YouTube, blogs, Twitter, and many other technologies, programs, sites, and venues—has affected many parts of our lives. So why wouldn't it also affect academic P&T? Facebook can negatively influence the way people, including those who will decide on your tenure bid, think about you. Problems can arise when professors share too much of their private lives with students, colleagues, and the rest of the online world.

In the prehistoric era of online social-interactive media—2000 to 2005—the debate over whether probationary faculty members should blog and participate in online social networking was binary: some argued yes, some said never. Now the discussion has shifted to "How do I do it safely?" or, more bluntly, "How do I do it without mucking up my tenure?" Let's review some ways that you can minimize the possibility that your blog, Facebook page, or Google results for your name might hurt your career track.

**Consider your "final" audience for P&T.** The people who will judge your tenure case were born at least two generations ago and began their professional careers long before blogging became commonplace. They grew up in an era when a diary was kept secret and revealed only posthumously. In their view, there ought to be a wall, not of postings, but of separation between work and home. Only in the rarest cases should professors share intimate details of their lives with students. Although some senior professors have adapted to the more open social media world of today, others possess stronger prejudices. To the latter colleagues, blogging is ridiculous, and anyone—including assistant professors—who blogs must be addled, wasting time, or unbearably self-infatuated. A faction, although they have adopted (perhaps reluctantly) the new technology themselves, still think of the Internet as a tool for the dissemination of professional products, not personal musings.

So when you assert on Facebook that you are "in the mood for loving," realize that the 65-year-old head of the P&T committee may not take it as a sign of your maturity as a scholar. And quite rightly he may be concerned about the effect of such openness, kidding around or not, on your students. Of course, there is a good chance that he might not see your intimate remarks, but you never know when somebody will point them out or print them out for him.

Also, consider that most independent bloggers are not hurt by a typo or two, but your situation may be different. If your blog posts are consistently badly spelled and ungrammatical, the impression of you as a professional, as a serious educator, and as a scholar is undermined. So you must never forget to maintain a good standard of prose for the masses . . . and the P&T committee.

Two cases illustrate the fallout of a bad Web persona. A social science department was hiring for an assistant professor, tenure-track position. As is now *de rigueur*, the chair of the search committee ran a Google scan on the top candidates. To her horror, the very first hit for one Ph.D. job-seeker was a picture of him downing Jell-O shots in what must have been a truly jovial grad student party. The caption read, "Rupert's first love: Party hearty!" The head of the search committee was looking for someone whose "first love" was research, so she dropped the exuberant fellow from her finalist list.

In the same search, another candidate showed up on Facebook in a similar *bon vivant* pose; luckily for her, the search committee dug deeper and realized the page belonged to someone else with the same name. (They had not seen her face-to-face before.) In this case, the true candidate had no Facebook page. During her campus visit, several members of the committee mentioned the almost fatal mix-up. The candidate thanked them and promptly put up a page that made clear her name and affiliation as well as featured a picture of her giving a lecture to fascinated-looking undergraduate students.

So taking steps to manage your virtual image is as important as managing your "face" in real life.

**Control your own content.** Facebook is a particularly dangerous weapon for self-injury because, more than with many other social-networking sites, it is so easy to share an embarrassing admission or offensive quip. When Facebook asks you, "What's on your mind?" the temptation may be strong to go right from musing, to typing, to clicking the "share" button: "Cristina is frustrated that her students can't write and don't seem to care" or "Cristina thinks her department head is dull, dull" or "Cristina's article has been rejected so many times she is thinking of quitting this stupid business."

You may daydream such thoughts, but Facebook virtually carves them in stone for others to goggle at or to pass on. My advice to both students and teachers is an echo of counsel made by Mark Twain and President Harry Truman in the "old media" age: Don't do or say anything that you would not want to see on the front page of the newspaper.

Controlling content also means being the final editor or filter of items under your aegis or even your name. I once gave several grad students the password to my own blog and permission to post items of political communication analysis, to which the blog is largely devoted. My many cautions to "stick to facts and reasoned insight" and not to get into name calling were disregarded by one of them, and I ended up deleting his post as quickly as I saw it. That didn't stop several other blogs quoting his nasty remarks as coming from *my* blog, as if it were my own editorial position.

**Professionalize your page, or create an alter ego.** The simplest way to make social media work for you in P&T is to restrict your use of it to professional content: blog about research and teaching in your field, and use Facebook to share updates on professional achievements such as article publications, speeches, and so on. Flickr or Picasa pictures might show off positive P&T moments such as your presenting at a conference or posing with students at graduation. Or make social media like YouTube augment your teaching with blog-enabled interactive assignments.

The only major drawback with maintaining a purely professional social media presence is that it's no fun. Certainly, there is intellectual satisfaction in blogging about a research finding, or sharing about a publication on Facebook, or tweeting about your pride in your students at commencement. But, in the case of Facebook, getting personal with friends about your life and theirs is what it's all about.

Two options can merge Facebook and other social media into both work and play. The first is toning down and self-censoring social media offerings to avoid the overly personal. You must certainly not release comments ("My dean has onion breath" or "My students are australopithecines") or pictures (of yourself or others in any state of dishabille

or inebriation) that will cause the P&T committee to believe you are
not a serious colleague. Self-censorship is proper. Remember the responsibility and maturity persona that you want to project.
Plan B is more drastic: create an alter ego via a pseudonym. A few
years ago, while researching a book on political blogging, I guest-
blogged under a nom de guerre at two political blogs. I learned quickly
that I didn't enjoy the ferocity of the venue, but those academics who
do can certainly find ways to hide their true identity. In fact, a number
of well-known pseudonymous bloggers have "come out" after receiving
tenure—and nobody, as far as I know, has demanded they lose their
tenure retroactively.

If you must vent online about your colleagues or students, research
how to create the most untraceable Web identity. Typical Web mas-
querade techniques have many holes in them. Blogging under a pseudonym is not *guaranteed* to give you cover. It is possible to out someone
either by a process of deduction—especially if he refers to events on
his campus—or with a little bit of Web-based sleuth work. I myself
was almost unmasked during one of my pseudonymous stints on a
political blog when one commenter narrowed down my university
from a reference I had made, even though I was not blogging about
academia at all. Luckily, he approved of my political ravings and so
kindly warned me about the potential leak.

Be aware also that anonymity and pseudonymity don't protect you
from police and lawyers. Slander, defame, or threaten your colleagues
or your dean, and they will find you out. (Of course, if you feel you
need to do such things, maybe you should get out of that employment
situation entirely.)

**Choose your "friends" carefully.** Screen the people on Facebook whom
you allow on your friends list. Avoid becoming friends with undergraduates in your classes. (Note: Explain your policy to students so it does not
come off as unfriendly to those who will fill out your course evaluations.)
Most faculty rightly feel leery about learning everything 18-year-olds are
doing and about their students knowing what they are doing.

Friends also can clash with friends and judge you by your virtual
company. I teach political communication and, over the years, have

made Facebook friends on the (very) left and (very) right. Sometimes I wince and wonder what they must think when they read my wall and see offensive (to them) posts by the other side. One professor had to dump some Facebook friends because they started rants that, while protected by the Constitution, made him look like a racist because he had allowed them on his page. And your friends can hurt your reputation as much as you can hurt it yourself: that embarrassing photo of you at a party or that impolitic remark you made about your department can become an unguided missile wandering about cyberspace ready to shoot down your good name.

**Don't get too personal . . . maybe.** One goal of your tenure-track years is to establish an image of seriousness, focus, and diligence. Two issues are at stake here.

First, avoid earning a reputation as someone who is overly consumed with affairs outside of work. One assistant professor used his Facebook page to dwell on a collecting hobby to the point where a senior faculty member (whom he had friended) asked, "You spend a lot of time on that hobby, don't you?" with the implication that it was perhaps too much time.

Second, senior professors grew up in an era when there was little mixing of the home and the workplace. Do you really want your colleagues to know, for example, that your "relationship status" has changed to "complicated"? Moreover, female faculty—as discussed earlier—especially in the sciences, have testified that they actively try to suppress "mommy talk" because they are wary that such discourse might contribute to a negative stereotype of them by senior male colleagues. Mommy imagery on Facebook may feed such unfair suspicions.

**Flood Google with positives.** Many people at different stages of life and career are worried about what is lurking and linking in cyberspace about them. As someone whose research area includes the effect of social media on our lives, I come across many examples of what might be called blogophobia.

I was interviewed by a publication for college students that focused on how both employers and admissions officers were increasingly using applicants' Web sites as part of background checks. Similarly, a young professor who served as faculty adviser to a sorority told me that she and the membership committee regularly denied entry to candidates who appeared on Flickr or elsewhere on the Web naked, drunk, or both. I spoke about blogs to a group of high school teachers and found their number-one fear was being "YouTubed"—that is, being provoked to lose their temper in class and then recorded for the world to mock via a cell-phone video. Recently an older professor, for the first time, did a Google search of his own name and was horrified to find some attacks on him by a disgruntled student on the latter's blog. He lamented to me, "I devote 40 years to scholarship and teaching, and then one guy who didn't get an 'A' brands me as evil on the Internet."

Attempts to remove offensive items by you and about you are rarely fully successful because there is no "complete delete" on the Web. Something you put up is always stored somewhere and may very well have been passed along. There is, however, a simple expedient. The key to avoiding the casual seeker stumbling onto something embarrassing or offensive about you is to make sure positive items make the first ten Google hits—and beyond. The prudent academic should try to insert professional items—op-eds, blog posts, and interviews that deal with research or teaching—into the Web stream. Eventually, the good crowds out the bad on Google shelf space.

**Inculcate the seniors.**  It is a stereotype based on reality to a high degree that social media, at first anyway, were a platform and a forum of expression for the young. Teenagers notoriously text-message several (even several hundreds of) times a day, but few grandparents do. For the assistant professor, the social media gap in age groups is a golden opportunity to (a) show what a good colleague you are, (b) demonstrate the professional utility of new media to older fellow faculty (such as those on the P&T committee!), and (c) be seen as a leader in the innovation of research and teaching.

Case in point: An assistant professor in a language department at a liberal arts college found herself in the following conversation with a near-retirement colleague. He claimed that the students were spending so much time interacting via the new media technologies, from text messaging to Facebook, that he was concerned that his lectures didn't reach them anymore. Basically, he was speculating as to whether his information delivery system was outmoded.

She argued, to the contrary, that talking about compelling subjects that you are passionate about is still an effective communication tool. But she tactfully suggested that he might augment his pedagogical toolkit with some social media. She helped him set up a class blog on which he could post general comments on readings and assignments and engage in cross-discussion with the students. It was a good deed that paid off for everyone, as the senior professor told her that his undergraduate charges seemed to be more interested in the class and looked upon him less as a dinosaur than they had before.

**Augment your teaching.** What students think of you affects your morale, your sense of belonging to the profession, and your progress on the tenure track. All universities and departments assert that student evaluations do not comprise the sole measure of pedagogical worthiness, but that 1 to 5 score, especially weighed over six years, is an influential indicator of your teaching performance. Social media in the classroom will not magically improve your skills or scores, but there are innovative ways to use them to connect with students and enliven the material. Investigate, via the research in educational technology and on teaching blogs and essays, what people have tried and perfected. Experiment, innovate, and even pioneer ways to marry new technology and old principles. The students will not only be impressed with your modernity but also—the key component in student evaluations—by how much "she cares about us."

Facebook represents a break from the early days of the Web when the seemingly glorious promise was of everyone interacting with everyone else. Two decades later, social media are more refined and targeted. We want to socialize with people we like and trust, those we respect and from whom we can glean valuable information. Today's tech-nimble academics will play a major role in shaping the definition and parameters of online interactivity to come. Smart young scholars will also grasp how such enterprising behavior can help their careers thrive as much as their online popularity.

## And in the End . . .

A Beatles song serves as a coda to a chapter about getting along with other academics: "In the end the love you take is equal to the love you make."

Nothing I advise here should interfere with the pursuit of excellence in research and teaching or with being a good person. There are cases in which people have gotten P&T who objectively did not deserve it based on their track record of achievement but who had cannily plugged into an old boys' network that carried them past the finish line. I have also seen and heard of well-qualified young scholars and teachers denied tenure because of "people issues," their own or those of others. But there is no contradiction between being a good scholar and a good teacher and being a good colleague; if you work at an institution that forces you to become a schemer, a backstabber, or a scoundrel to get P&T, then you should be looking elsewhere to get P&T.

In sum, understanding the human relations aspect of academia is crucial for your success, but it doesn't replace the work listed in the job profile for which you were hired. Doing good is also good for *you*. Among the analects attributed to Confucius is a piece of advice that has reverberated in different forms and from different prophetic authors through the millennia; today it is widely discussed as the "principle of reciprocity."[13] As stated in the original (in translation), it is:

> As for Goodness—you yourself desire rank and standing; then help others to get rank and standing. You want to turn your own merits to account; then help others to turn theirs to account—in fact, the ability to take one's own feelings as a guide—that is the sort of thing that lies in the direction of Goodness.[14]

In other words, you should help others as you *wish* others would help you, and helping others will indeed often help you if you have the right attitude about it. Not everyone gets back what they give. If you base helping other people, like students or peers, on expectations of rewards or gratitude, you will be disappointed. And the older you get in our business the more the "no good deed goes unpunished" axiom seems like reality.

On the other hand, some of the best, most accomplished, successful professors I know have the most generous hearts, and as far as I am aware they don't stay up at night grinding their teeth because the world has not paid them back adequately. They seem to genuinely enjoy being decent human beings. If you can inculcate that quality in yourself, you will have greater satisfaction in your career than in practically anything else you accomplish.

# CHAPTER 4

# The Balancing Act—
# Self, Family, and Tenure

᛫᛫᛫

The next two chapters deal with parts of the mosaic of career advancement in academia that are just as vital as good relations with peers. Here, I identify key issues in the balancing of self, home-family, and work—although, as noted earlier, on the tenure track an imbalance toward work is normal and necessary. The next chapter covers student relations and how they play a role in P&T as well as your job satisfaction.

Now, I have no statistic to prove that academic life is harder on families than, say, joining the Navy. But if you grow up in academia, you do note that certain trends go beyond anecdote and the frightening icons of *Who's Afraid of Virginia Woolf?* My father once observed that he was one of the few professors of his generation that he knew who had not divorced his first wife to marry a graduate student or a departmental secretary. Over and over you see strains, stresses, and fractures in partnership and marriages as the workloads and expectations for tenure for new faculty (and worries about not getting tenure) rise ever higher.[1]

Of equal fascination is that the relation of one's personal life to one's work life varies in the mind of the beholder. At one conference, a graduate student asked a celebrated senior researcher what was the secret of his success. The reply was "childlessness." The story may be apocryphal, but the sentiment is not—professor-parents regularly lament, albeit almost always glibly, about their "son costing them a book." An industry of articles discusses the balancing (or fire-torch juggling) act that comprises being on the tenure track as well as on the mommy-wife, husband-father, or even caregiver-to-elderly-parents track. The old days of the male professor focusing entirely on his work while the at-home or secretarial wife did all the housework and child care are finished.

On the other hand, as discussed in detail later, "the kids" are an often employed reason or excuse to exit a faculty meeting early or to miss a deadline. A single colleague of mine told me that she thought I was more productive because I *had* children: "You are more grounded, you see more what you are working to support."

The point is that younger faculty of the modern era, male and female, want a personal life: they want to date, fall in love, and perhaps have children and certainly interact with those children as they grow up. They don't, as I stated in the introduction, expect to have it all, but they do hope that getting tenure will not destroy their happiness outside the office. They do not think, in sum, that the price of success in academia should be unhappy loved ones, unhealthy bodies, and unfulfilled souls.

Such wishes are moral and ethical; they are even achievable. Many of us in academia do try to balance home and work, and we encourage others to do so. For example, a faculty member at a midwestern school considered taking on an administrative position within his unit. He was qualified for the post, and he was mature and responsible, but he had two children who pursued a dizzying schedule of viola lessons, ballet practices, and soccer games. He wondered whether he could take care of both his lives. His dean was encouraged rather than dismayed by the professor's concerns: she did not want anyone working for her who neglected his family. Indeed, a good husband, wife, father, mother, partner, or caregiver can still be a good colleague.

Still, *how* do you put such ideals into practice, especially when you might find yourself in an all-work culture and a grinding tenure track?

## Family Matters

As discussed in the chapter about being a doctoral student, the balancing of home and office responsibilities (and knowing when imbalances are acceptable) begins long before you take up the tenure track.

Even if you are a single graduate student, you have relatives, friends, hobbies, interests, and a body and mind to keep healthy. For any of us, but especially for the probationary faculty member, the role of family in our lives, and how others perceive family as related to our work, can affect our careers. *Talking* about family—that is, the use of "family" as a topic of conversation, as an excuse, or even as a target within academic culture in general and P&T in particular—can be problematic. Let's begin with cases drawn both from faculty I know and from a number of *Chronicle of Higher Education* forums and blog writers. In one narrative, a female interviewee felt ambushed by the "do you have kids?" question and contested its legality; unsurprisingly, she was not offered a position. In several other columns, writers advised female faculty to avoid the "F" word altogether in job interviews and to suppress family talk on the job.

Their rationale is that a double standard exists, especially in the physical sciences. A senior male professor feels free to show off pictures of his grandkids and boast of building a tree house for them without fear of not being taken seriously as a scholar; however, a junior female faculty member suspects that lamenting her young son's erratic sleep habits will brand her as a "mommy tracker." The argument for or against using the F word is not binary (yes/no, on/off) in many other situations in academia.

Here are some family-realistic protocols. They are based on the three-P premise that while academia is an individualistic calling, academics are also colleagues and employees with professional responsibilities.

**Don't overplay the family card as an excuse.** Families are ready-made reasons to evade unwanted work or campus commitments. What academic parent isn't tempted to blow off a late curriculum committee meeting by saying, not necessarily truthfully, "Sorry, I have to pick up my kids from school"? But having children is not a "get out of service duties" or "let out class early" or "be late for a deadline" free card. As a childless assistant professor once queried bluntly, "Is my time less valuable because I didn't breed?" Or, as another single professor with two parents with Alzheimer's disease argued, nowadays most of us are caregivers of one kind or another. So while there will be instances when you must commit to family over duty to your students or colleagues, you owe the latter a pledge to arrange your life to minimize those collisions. Furthermore, having a reputation of not overly using family as the reason to escape a work commitment means that your colleagues might be more understanding when you have to.

**Don't earn an "overly family-oriented" reputation.** Try to limit talk about family to modest quantities and explicitness. This advice applies to more of us than just to young, female, tenure-track biologists. A language scholar—gray-haired, male, and well published—regularly updated all his colleagues about his young adopted daughter's adorable antics and school achievements. The e-mailed pictures and long digressions before, during, and after faculty meetings were apparently not enough for this proud papa: he dropped by people's offices to make sure no one lived in ignorance of the precocious moppet's many talents. Finally, his colleagues started avoiding him, even for collaborating on research. The price of coauthorship was too high when it involved listening to a third grader's poem of the day, every day. In general, appreciate that nobody loves (or wants to see and hear about) your kids as much as you do. Family photos and "I love you, Daddy" artwork in the office are fine; slide shows of potty training are not.

**Err on the side of an image of devotion to work.** For the doctoral candidate on the job market as well as the probationary academic on the tenure track, there is a default mode in the family-talk conundrum: devotion to work. You don't have to be anti-family, but at the end of the day giving off signals that all you care about is your woodshop, your five cats, and being a Boy Scout troop leader gains you less than it detracts. No need to say, "I never see my kids because I am in the lab all night and day." But having a reputation as a conscientious worker who understands that, especially during the tenure-track years, the personal must to some extent be sacrificed for the professional is almost never a negative.

Academic culture may be evolving to the point where, in some future time, no one need worry that admitting to having a rambunctious toddler or a mother in failing health will count against you at a job interview. Even so, for now, balancing family, research, teaching, and service does not mean that the scale will always be horizontally even. In these tough times, we should be grateful that we are in a profession that offers more family accommodations than most. All the more reason for each of us, especially the tenure tracker, not to abuse the privileges of that freedom.

### Is Your Spouse Hurting Your Career?

Self-evidently many academics marry other academics. No guarantee of extra stability or understanding is offered by a professor pairing. But what about "mixed" marriages? In some cases, with no malice or sabotage intended, the non-academic partner's behavior or ideas can undermine or even cripple the scholar's career because of mutual ignorance and mistaken assumptions. When the relationship is failing, the academic's work can be but one collateral casualty of a wider war.

First, some context: Examine dissertations published through the 1970s, and you will find a high number of acknowledgments "to my wife for typing this manuscript through several editions." These days, although most academics, male and female, do their own keyboarding, dissertations and scholarly books regularly credit "my husband, Enrique, who endured this project" or "my partner, Tyrion, for his tireless support." Come tenure time, the celebration party typically includes a paean to "the real hero who made this possible."

Almost always, the kudos are plausible and sincere. Not many successful academics achieved their career milestones *despite* their partners. So clearly, the non-academic spouse can play positive roles, from confidante to cheerleader to tear-drier.

But some mixed partnerships have no such benefits. Why?

One reason could be unacknowledged ignorance about our line of work. Sometimes we forget or don't know how to explain that academia is idiosyncratic. You can make comparisons between what happens in faculty meetings and the behaviors and procedures of the boardroom, the manufacturing plant, the law office, the medical clinic, or the cubicle warren. But getting a Ph.D. degree, producing scholarly research, navigating the tenure track, teaching at the college and university level, and laboring toward full professorship and beyond subsume singular mindsets and means of conduct.

Non-academics, for example, often have a different sense of proper "work" time. In one case, a young assistant professor was struggling to complete her research agenda. The tenure clock ticked and her frustration grew. She could not get any work done at home and was under pressure not to stay at the office beyond "the normal 9 to 5," as her husband put it. Her children and spouse were not being spiteful but simply assumed that once in the home geospace, she should convert to wife and mother. In turn, she hated to disappoint their expectations but chafed at the lost hours. Frustration begat resentment which begat lack of focus which begat a floundering career.

Furthermore, academics and non-academics may have differing views of productivity. A normal office worker may define it in terms of money: a big raise or major sales of a product. By contrast, a highly successful assistant professor in some fields might point to a single journal article for all her efforts in a *year*. To wit, one young scholar showed his partner his annual report that cited two papers he had had accepted for publication at top journals. A colleague in the field would have recognized that achievement as champagne-poppingly impressive. But the partner, a software manager at an information-technology firm, burst into laughter and said, "You professors get away with murder. If I accomplished that little in a year I would be canned."

Non-academic spouses can also be befuddled or bemused by the P&T process. In most businesses, there are multiple variations and gradations of advancement. But an academic career involves only two key promotions, the first of which—tenure—is literally make or break. If you are denied tenure, you typically have no chance of getting another position at the same university. Yet I have heard of non-academic spouses telling their partners, "I meet deadlines all the time; tenure is just a bigger one, right?" or "Too bad you didn't get tenure. But you can always try again next year!"

Office politics is also a source of confusion between mixed couples. Yes, the academic department can be a place of discord, backstabbing, power plays, and dissimulation, but that doesn't mean that most academics welcome such behaviors or that those behaviors can prove beneficial to a career. One administrator described a well-qualified job candidate who "talked himself out of a job." The candidate blurted out all sorts of downright weird demands and suspicions, raising objections to any request and basically treating the job offer like a hardball business-labor contract negotiation. The administrator gave up and said, "Maybe you should find another job elsewhere, because we can't make you happy." Then the source of the candidate's tactics emerged: he had been "advised" to be aggressive by his lawyer spouse, who was indeed a specialist in labor negotiations.

Although it is obvious that an antagonistic and demeaning spouse can hurt your work, conversely a cheerleader and fierce partisan can undermine your progress toward P&T as well. There is a line between being on your side and being an enabler for your obstinacy and obtuseness. It doesn't help you if every time you go home to complain about campus politics, your partner reassures you that you are blameless and intones, "Those bastards are out to get you." Many career wounds that academics suffer are self-inflicted; we need someone to love and support us but also to suggest alternative scenarios to the "poor pitiful me" lament. One professor explained that her husband listens patiently to her campus-driven frustrations but then, at some point, asks, "So what was your role in all this?"

Many spousal-induced career problems in academia are rooted in miscommunication. The spouse is not intentionally sinking your career but simply does not know how best to assist it. But sometimes an intervention is possible. In the case of the young assistant professor previously mentioned, for instance, it became clear that the main problem in her lack of progress toward tenure was her husband, or rather their joint inability to define what her career required to flourish.

He was an office worker who, in the classic formula, believed "you don't bring work home with you" and didn't particularly see the value of her research, assuming it was "just a way to make a living." She, like most academics, was not able to complete work at the office, what with the bustle of students and distractions of minutiae.

I couldn't help myself: I finally cornered the gentleman in question at a party. I got him talking about his job and eventually asked, "Isn't it funny how different your wife's job is from yours?" I then enumerated all that our trade demanded of us, emphasizing the requirement for undisturbed hours at home for thinking, reading, and writing and a partner who believes in what we are devoting our lives to study, with an understanding of the particular nature of the sacrifices we need to make and that our loved ones need to accept.

Conversations between the two of them, after that night, resulted in a new alignment in mutual expectations and supportiveness. Indeed, there is research that shows that simply talking over with one's family the scope and demands of the workplace can improve the efficiency of one's labors.[2]

Which is exactly the point: All of us, when we commit to the academic life, need to be candid with our non-academic life-partners and negotiate a reasonable plan that furthers our relationship as well as our careers.

Another consideration faced by more and more academics is the effect of one's *academic* spouse on one's career. I know quite a few higher-education couples who are in the same department, more who are in the same field, and many who teach at the same university. In fact, having an academic spouse can sometimes help you get a job in cases of hiring as a "spousal accommodation." Nevertheless, once you are in the door, especially if you are both in the same unit, there is a basic rule of engagement for navigating the people-and-politics issues that others may have with you and that you may have with others: maintain professional distance.

I joked once with an academic couple I knew who were both professors in the same unit that they should have at least one loud argument about curriculum or course scheduling at a faculty meeting each year. I don't actually advocate such a tactic, but it is critical for academic couples not to be—or be perceived to be—an indistinguishable unified *political* entity. Some faculty already hold suspicions and prejudices that academic couples will form their own snug voting block or faction. A female professor related that a colleague talking to her about a controversial departmental bylaw change told her, in effect, "Well, since you favor the measure, that means your husband's vote is all sewn up, so I've got two votes against me already." Even if you do agree on academic matters all the time, you should exude an aura of individuality, that at least it's possible that you will disagree.

One final principle to maintain is that no one—your dean, students, or colleagues—should assume that just because you're married, when they talk to one of you no separate conversation needs to be had with the other or, worse, that any confidence shared with one professor is always relayed at home to the partner.

## Is P&T Making You Sick?

A tenured physics professor still describes the nights during his probationary period when he would wake up sweating and anxious. He is not alone, of course. It is rather surprising that medical and psychological diagnostic manuals have not identified a "P&T syndrome," complete with familiar symptoms that every assistant professor has manifested to either a minor or a career-ending degree.

The P&T syndrome may be normal, but its frequency and commonplace nature do not make it more survivable by the sufferer. I'll address some of the actions you can take to relieve P&T syndrome, either your own case or that of those you befriend, love, or mentor.

First, a major caveat: My doctorate is in mass communications, so my focus here will be on milder forms of P&T syndrome. Depression, as we have learned in the last few decades, is a genuine killer. Assistant professors and those who care about them should not think that persistent deep feelings of worthlessness and sadness and physical symptoms such as chest pains must always be rooted in something as fleeting as the tenure track. So if you suspect that you are really sick, treat it seriously and get help.

But if you feel the tenure track is running you down, mentally or physically, without there being an organic or psychological stimulus of greater threat, then there is good news. It begins with the realization that being miserable does not have to be the normal state of the probationary faculty member.

I tried an experiment that I would like to see replicated more widely, perhaps by clinical psychologists in laboratory settings. One semester, around the time of my third year review, I was feeling particularly anxious about a paper that I was working on. I felt I was making no headway on it, that I would not get it published and was going to see several months of effort go to waste. I stepped back and did something that appealed to my sense of the absurd: I deleted my data and all the drafts of my paper and did everything possible to completely forget about it. I spent the rest of that semester focusing on my teaching and my service, and ruminating on some other projects I had considered starting.

Incredibly, it all worked out. My yearly report was positive. My student evaluations for the semester-of-my-sloth were markedly higher than the previous one, when I had been sweating about the paper. And I had the summer to make revisions in the final draft of a book manuscript that saw publication the next year. Now, a decade or so later, I have forgotten the precise topic of that paper and have no particular interest in reclaiming it. I found that the cause of my distress was acute and identifiable, not vague and chronic. My quasi-experiment on myself suggests that the goal of self-help in an academic career is not to turn you into a "happy wanderer"; rather, it is to arrest, deflect, or reorient the gloom-and-doom attitude that, far from helping propel you along the tenure track, is actually hurting your progress.

**Avoid banging into immovable objects.** Don't let pride, pigheadedness, or frustration sap you of the strength to abandon a project that has turned out to be a losing proposition. In poker terms, cut your losses and walk away from the table. An English professor described working on a book project and finding that his creativity was waning so that he despaired of ever finishing. At last, he decided to just give up. He put the manuscript in a file and forced himself to move on to another project. Years later, some other readings reawakened his interest so that he was able to pick up the manuscript on a new tack and finish it. On the other hand, quite a number of junior faculty slave away on some major project that is not returning their sustained engagement with the publications that are the coin of a successful P&T bid. Start something that can be finished and published in the time you have, and save your labors of Hercules for after tenure.

**Adopt positive distractions and reward systems.** Distractions from teaching, research, and service have both positive and negative aspects. It is useful for the up-and-coming faculty member to have a hobby or other interests that spark the creative juices and rejuvenate the mind. On the other hand, I question whether anyone on the tenure track can or should expect to have a full, rich, and rewarding personal life for those six years of intense and focused effort. A younger friend once told me that his tenure-track years in a tiny liberal arts college "in the middle of a cornfield" were a terrific career boost because he had nothing else to do but teach and type and watch HBO.

You can also create a reward system. When I was a doctoral student, a friend and I tried to come up with an incentive program to finish chapters on our respective dissertations. I needed a positive reward. Every time I finished a chapter, my friend would take me to dinner at a fine restaurant. She, on the other hand, found punishment to be greater incentive to data analysis and keyboarding. So we set dates for her to finish chapters, and if she did not complete them I was to make a small donation in her name to a political organization that she loathed. Most of the time our systems worked, although I think another factor was our mutual encouragement and desire to avoid failing our agreed-upon tests.

Whatever your character, a problem we academics often face is that our accomplishments have nebulous feedback. Yes, most of us do our research, teaching, and service for its own sake and not because we expect ticker-tape parades and showers of lucre. We teach a class well one semester, and a month later we get back an envelope with some numbers on it that tell us we did a good job. We publish an article in a journal, and maybe a few people pat us virtually on the back via e-mail. Only rarely and only for long-term achievements are there many real, large, and prestigious prizes offered. The average academic does not start building a trophy case until the middle and later parts of his or her career.

So quite a few young and middle-rank faculty I know have found it worthwhile to create their own systems of recompense (and sometimes reprimand). I like the one of the language professor who picked out from a catalog some modestly expensive porcelains and promised herself to buy one if she achieved her goals for a semester. If she did not, however, she would have to give away one of the pieces already in her collection.

**Don't be the giving tree.** The saddest instance of dysfunctionality on the tenure track is when young scholars and teachers literally sacrifice themselves out of a job. In research universities, the typical scenario is as follows. A new tenure tracker loves her subject and her charges. She is a terrific teacher and indeed pours a lot of energy into her class preparations, creates many interesting assignments, grades them thoroughly, offers unlimited time for student consultation, stays in her office, door wide open 9 to 5, and then is denied tenure because she was unable to produce enough research. As detailed in the sections on time management and "saying no," if you give too much of yourself or focus too much on any one part of your job, the other parts will suffer. In a sense, then, a good tenure-track professor must have some degree of healthy selfishness. It's not all about you, but it's not all about "them" either.

**Create a second life.** A final thought: The academic life, at least according to popular culture, is one of leisure and banter interspersed with a few hours of off-the-cuff teaching. For instance, the character Gary on the late-1980s television show *thirtysomething* was an assistant professor of English literature with a large, beautiful office. Research, teaching, and service were invisible components of a lifestyle suffused with love-making and bicycling. (Reality did intrude a bit when he was denied tenure.) More recently on the situation comedy *Community*, the highly addled faculty seem to spend little or no time preparing for class—a true fantasy compared with the weighty and lengthy teaching and advising loads of real community college professors.

In fact, young scholars and teachers today face the opposite problem: they often feel they have little or no life outside of the office and classroom.

Although the demands of P&T should not be minimized, career obsession is both a psychological and a practical mistake. You need more than one life.

David Heenan, a management scholar, makes the intellectual case for having multiple lives—career, personal, communal, spiritual, and even artistic—in his 2002 book *Double Lives*.[3] He documents how some of history's most successful (and busy) people found it both necessary and enriching to devote time to alternate forms and forums of creativity that seemed, on the surface, to have nothing to do with their more famous vocations.

Winston Churchill, for example, besides his roles as husband, father, historian, commentator, scholar, politician, warlord, and statesman, painted (mostly landscapes and still lifes) and laid bricks. His visual artistry and masonry have never been as well regarded as his political or literary accomplishments, but the time he spent spreading colors on canvas and mortar on brick gave him great satisfaction, clarity of mind, and inspiration. Heenan argues that even those of us whose career ambitions are on a lower scale than saving the free world should find a similar "second life."

In contrast, the stress of conflicts over time, focus, and needs for the tenure tracker undermines both careers and personal lives. In trying to satisfy every demand for our attention, we are in danger of leaving them all unfulfilled. But reasonable alternatives do exist that can keep you from having no life outside of work, or from being denied tenure because you were overwhelmed by family obligations.

Be candid about what you need to achieve your career goals. Explain the importance of your ambitions and negotiate, especially with your partner, an equitable division of labor.

Accept that you will not be there for everything for everyone. Certainly, a reasonable administrator will accommodate an assistant professor who, for example, cannot schedule classes on late Tuesday and Thursday afternoons because that's when he takes his elderly mother to physical therapy. But on the other side—and trust me on this—your kids will not grow up to hate you if you don't attend every soccer game and ballet recital. Paradoxically, a constructive step is to take Heenan's advice and discover a second life—that is, a new creative outlet. It is counterintuitive but true that devoting (reasonable) time to pottery or model trains can make you more productive in your work life.

The general point is that doctoral studies and the tenure track are unavoidably and justifiably times where the personal must be sacrificed in part for the professional. You can't have it all; no one ever did or does. But neither is the prize of tenure worth it if you feel pressured in fact or in fantasy to surrender all hope of personal happiness and fulfillment.

# CHAPTER 5

# Student Relations

Student relations are similar to family relations. At some small colleges, faculty are indeed encouraged to practically adopt students, with barbecues and birthday parties and old-fashioned *in loco parentis* mentoring. Those of us at public research universities befriend our advisees. Conversely, tensions in student relations mirror those for family. As an assistant professor, I went through a period where, under great self-induced stress about finishing a book, I began to resent the intrusion of my students into my work time. No matter that by contract, at least 40 percent of my work time was supposed to be about students. I was at a research university where good teaching was encouraged, but nobody who did not perform *very* well in research got tenure. I started chafing at the grading, the office hours. *The book, the book, must finish the book! Why are all these people conspiring to get in my way?!*

The feeling passed after that book was published. I resolved to find a balance between teaching and research. I realized that, for the sake of honor if not tenure hopes, most academics must find a way to teach well. But just as in relations with fellow faculty and deans, student relations are about managing your public persona as well as concrete actions.

So, lest you fall into the trap I did, keep in mind the following:

- Don't get along with students and you will suffer in the "teaching" category of your promotion and tenure (P&T) evaluation.
- Don't get along with students and you will be stressed, which can't help you with the other parts of your life and job. (This is a

significant problem. In a survey of undergraduate educators by the National Opinion Research Center, "student preparation and commitment" was listed by the highest number of respondents as their primary stressor.[1])

Last and little discussed, the tenure track is a novel phase in your career when you will be judged by people (such as the seniors on the P&T committee or peers in other institutions who may be outside reviewers of your P&T packet) *not just on your own performance in research, teaching, and service but on the performance of your students or protégés.* They are, in marketing terms, an extension of your brand, the imprimatur of your reputation. By grading, advising, or writing letters of reference, for instance, you are giving your word of honor, your signed and dated pledge as a colleague and a professional, that in your estimation somebody has certain attributes, qualities, and levels of skill that will lead her to be successful somewhere else, no longer under your guardianship.

That your student brand is an extension of your own is illustrated by the plight of a rhetoric-composition assistant professor at a regional state university. She struggled in her first year, teaching several introductory classes. She was stressed and distressed at the low student evaluations and frustrated in finding the best way to teach the material. But adding salt to these wounds was the comment passed on as originating from a senior faculty member who complained that her students, when they showed up in his advanced class, weren't prepared enough. She was grappling, thus, with the expectations not only of students but with those of seniors.

In her case, the beginning of a solution started with practicality and humility. Rather than waiting for the senior professor to complain to her directly, she went to him and said in effect, "I want to provide the highest quality pipeline of students to your class. I'd love to get your advice on revising my syllabi and assignments." She also consulted the teaching resource center on campus and other accomplished veteran pedagogues. Her teaching and evaluation scores both improved, but also the senior faculty were impressed by her stick-to-it, egoless self-improvement.

## Thwarting Misbehavior in the Classroom

After giving a midterm examination to a large lecture class during my tenure-track years, I briefly considered quitting academia. The stimulus was the declaration by a student—incensed at my "unfair" questions, which he characterized as "way too hard"—that I was a "jerk." The young man spoke loudly enough for me to hear. I was furious. Of course, like any educator, I've had students complain privately (in my office, on the phone, or through e-mail) that I am unfair, too rigorous, and a variety of other bad things. I never thought, however, that I would be reviled publicly in a university classroom.

I read the student the riot act, stressing the importance of respect for teachers, and generally denounced his bad behavior to the heavens. I'm not sure whether the other students were more alarmed at the young man's rudeness or at my red-faced diatribe. I did regain my composure enough to let him complete the exam. I never felt so bad about myself or my teaching skills.

There is a social-cultural context to such behavior. The media world in which most American young people spend many hours a day is the antithesis of the traditional classroom, or even what we used to call "adult comportment." We are competing with instant messaging and instant game controllers, and we are receiving instant judgments: every lecture is in competition with frantic special effects movies, YouTube videos, or World of Warcraft battles. Jeff Powell—a Duke professor of law and divinity, and recipient of the university's 2002 Scholar/Teacher of the Year Award—summed up our challenge: if we don't entertain our students, "then they tune out. They also begin judging us right away."

Realizing that students have power in the classroom is a cognitive leap for many faculty. Certainly when I began teaching, I saw the classroom as my savanna, and myself as at the top of the food chain. The students owed me respect, by golly. It took me some time to accept that, from their point of view, the situation is quite different. One of my best and brightest students told me, "You have to win us over, not the reverse. You have to tell us what the game plan is and why we should follow it." In short, persuade rather than command.

Besides getting students to go along with our plans for a course, we must convince them that maintaining order in the classroom is in their best interest. Robert V. Friedenberg, a professor of communication at Miami University in Ohio, makes a dollars-and-cents pitch for decorum, telling his class that "each student in the room has paid more for this class than for any concert ticket or sporting-event ticket that they have ever purchased."

Other approaches are possible. For example, graduate students in the humanities may appreciate a philosophical discussion of tactics to promote classroom etiquette, including comments about how they might handle unruly students when they start teaching. In some disciplines, it may make sense to tell students that they must behave in class as they will eventually have to in a business office.

But offering practical reasons for being civil is not sufficient. We have to win students' hearts as well as their minds.

Every professor probably has some pedagogical handicaps. By admitting that the problems exist and dealing with them, we demonstrate not professional failure or surrender to the students but pure pragmatism. If students believe we care about them, they are less likely to behave badly in our courses.

The litmus test of a professor's caring is fairness—what my angry student accused me of lacking. People who suspect that they aren't being treated fairly often rebel through bad behavior, minor and major. We can demonstrate our fairness by explaining why we put certain books on the reading list, why we make particular assignments, and why mutual respect is a necessary part of education. Students may accept tough professors, but they do not tolerate what they think is unfair.

Dealing with infractions is the other side of the coin of handling misbehavior. Students learn what is acceptable in class from what other students get away with. For example, once a young lady asked to speak to me after class. She told me that she had had trouble concentrating because the student next to her had been watching a movie on a laptop.

I realized that I was partly at fault. My list of classroom do's and don'ts on the syllabus had not caught up to such a form of inattention—I had noted that reading was distracting, but movie watching had not occurred to me. I commended the young lady for her interest in focusing on her studies and suggested she sit farther away from the other student in the future. Then, in the next lecture, I observed aloud that it was unfair to other students to distract them in class in any way; their "right to learn" was being violated. I said that if someone wanted to watch a movie, I could set aside a section of the room, and perhaps even open a concession stand. I got some laughs; I also received no further complaints about movie watching.

Humor helps. I try to "punish" most low-level misbehavior with genial embarrassment. I might give a student who rushes into class late, slamming the door, a gentle quiz on how tough his day has been or directions to a vacant seat. Most students will do anything to avoid being the butt of class merriment; I find few repeat offenders.

Of course, there is no magic elixir that will make students be civil to us and each other. Most undergraduates are, after all, very young, and still exploring how to behave. Their brain capacities are developing in crucial ways—judgment, foresight, emotional maturity, assessment of risk, etc. They are seldom malicious or consciously trying to undermine teachers or distract their peers. They just are growing up in a coarse and chaotic culture. And most of them, if they come from middle-class backgrounds, are on their own for the first time without the constant protection and troubleshooting of their fixer/manager/personal assistant/helicopter parents.

That was the case with the student who called me a jerk. He continued to attend class without further incident. I referred him to the Dean of Students to referee our mutual problem. A few weeks before the end of the semester, I found a handwritten note of apology from him in my mailbox. I believe it was sincere and not prompted by fear—he was an A student. When I saw him next, I shook his hand and pronounced the case closed as far as I was concerned.

It was, I hope, a learning experience for both of us. Students will always misbehave periodically. So will professors. But as educators we have a duty to encourage the best behavior in our pupils. That task is as integral to our job (and getting tenure) as the content of any lecture. Show you care, and explain why you are fair, and many problems will be averted.

## Supervising Your Student Assistants

Consider the juxtaposition in position when you become an assistant professor. You are officially a faculty member, but mere weeks ago you defended your dissertation. Among the rewards and challenges that might arrive at your door even before the semester starts: your first teaching and research assistants.

The P&T system, like academia itself, reflects its ancient and medieval origins in style and substance. At its heart is a guild that takes in apprentices, tests them in the craft at the assistant-professor rank, and then, if it finds them worthy, offers them associate and then full membership. But the apprentice also has his own apprentices. A novice assistant professor of biology at a major research university might suddenly find herself leading several graduate students and post-docs in a big lab. Conversely, a sociologist, two years away from tenure, may be assigned a graduate student to help him finish a book. Or an associate professor at a community college might have a five-hour-a-week undergraduate assistant to help with a curriculum project.

You may be guaranteed an assistant as part of your hiring contract or provided one each semester, depending on resource availability. Your assistant may be passionately interested in your (mutual) research, or be an undergraduate from another department working for minimum wage and holding a "this is just my job" attitude.

For any of those cases and many other variations, a good assistant, one who really helps advance your teaching and research, is valuable to an almost immeasurable degree. I still recall how, caught in the haze of my new job, I was fortunate to find a wonderful master's student to help complete my first book. She intuitively located information, organized it, and even helped find patterns in the archival data I was studying. Finishing that book without her seems impossible to ponder.

However, my relationships with some other assistants, either because of my poor supervision or their own foibles, or both, turned sour and unproductive. There was the teaching assistant who "forgot" to turn in my students' final exams at the scoring center, so I ended up submitting several hundred grades late. Another was so bored by the content-analysis coding I asked him to do that he fudged many of the answers. He and I parted ways early in the semester.

Clearly, good management of your research and teaching assistants can affect your future, and theirs. To that end, some common rules apply.

First, a fundamental precept: In times of tight budgets, consider yourself lucky to have an assistant at all. Someone—the taxpayers, a grant agency, an endowment, or the university—is paying for your assistants, no matter how much you feel you earned them. Therefore, you are under a legal and ethical obligation to supervise students who, while you may consider them protégés or even friends, are employees.

Problems arise, as was detailed at length in the chapter on doctoral education, when a faculty member, a student, or both consider an assistantship not to be a "real job." In my various administrative appointments, when I have been responsible for handing out assistantships to other faculty members, I have stressed to all parties that they are mutually responsible for the outcome of the professional relationship.

If at all possible, try to interview candidates for assistantships. It is hard to tell from a résumé how someone will work out. Graduate assistants with an outstanding record—having earned a prestigious scholarship, for example—may turn out to be problematic when put to work grading undergraduate papers. A colleague in a scientific field described such junior stars as "thinking they deserve the Nobel Prize right now" and so are unwilling to wash the beakers and feed the rats. On the other hand, a shy, minimum-wage undergraduate may become a dynamo in the archives if properly trained and rewarded.

An interview could help identify some potential landmines. Be as specific as possible about the nature of the work, the deadlines, and the daily schedule. Outline if on-the-job training (in, say, a software program or a data-entry technique) will be necessary. Don't just note the students' verbal responses. Body language and mood are key indicators, too. Do they seem attentive, tuned in to what you are trying to accomplish? A successful graduate teaching assistant may need to be upbeat and outgoing to supervise discussion sections of your large lecture course. Then again, research assistants who will spend all of their time cranking out statistics might be taciturn but highly efficient.

You also need to work out a contract that goes beyond your college's "20 hours a week for $10 an hour" or "full ride RA" description. Specify in writing measurable outcomes for the week, month, or semester and how they will be gauged. A wall chart tracking the progress of your project, for example, will be a useful tool for both of you.

Another critical preliminary step is to make sure your assistants are aware of, and understand, all university rules and codes pertaining to their employment, especially those affecting safety and privacy rights. Many institutions have special training workshops or certification programs for assistants. At the end of the day, however, you need to confirm that your assistants are in compliance with the rules covering the handling of lab equipment, human subjects, student files and records, and so on.

As the work proceeds, assess the project and give feedback. A biologist described how his graduate assistant had consistently done poor work for the entire sixteen weeks of the semester. Busy with other projects, however, he did not actually check her until the final days of the term, so he didn't find out about the difficulties until it was too late to fix anything, and too embarrassing to report it.

Besides inattention, a major factor in failed assistantships (or supervision) is dysfunctional niceness. An assistant professor from a humanities department lamented, "When I get lazy or distracted assistants, I let them get away with it. I can't bring myself to scold them or enact any real punishments." Here is where age proximity can be an inhibitor to tight management. You don't want to be perceived as an old meanie, so you tend to overlook problems and poor work, even at the expense of your own project. Sometimes older, more mature (but not necessarily more competent) assistants can actually intimidate you into silence.

But failing to correct difficulties as they are happening is not only bad for your projects, classes, and career but also for the system itself. Some graduate students may complain to other faculty members that while they worked long hours at a difficult task, another assistant was doing nothing for his paycheck. The senior professors who judge you at P&T time may take note. And the graduate assistants are getting a poor lesson that may undermine their careers.

A complicating factor is, of course, that assistants are students. They have to study for exams, their grandmothers fall ill, their love lives will go awry. The supervisor must judge whether excusing one or two absences or blown deadlines will lead to more of the same. You should be humane and empathic, but at some point you may also have to be tough, and, at a further point, you may have to issue an ultimatum. If all that fails, then a professional divorce is the final option. You can add kind phrases and regrets, but in the end you need to be firm. This is, after all—no matter how friendly—a business relationship. No "giving trees" allowed!

The "no good deed goes unpunished" rule applies, unfortunately. Problem assistants rarely solve their own problems. Slacker management does not cure slacker labor. And sometimes having no assistant is better than having one who only aggravates you.

At the other extreme, asking too much from an assistant can be as bad as asking too little. Guard against adopting unrealistic standards. I mentioned the solid-gold research assistant with whom I was blessed early in my career. Ultimately, of course, she graduated. I had adjustment problems for years afterward because so few other assistants performed to her level. It took me a good while to accept that she was an outlier at the right end of the bell curve. Over time, I learned that overseeing most graduate assistants requires as much effort from me as from them. Few assistants are born lazy, inattentive, and sloppy: it's more likely that their supervisors failed to take the time and effort to consider the best ways to prepare, motivate, and manage them.

The key is to make a plan, write it out, agree on it, and faithfully and diligently execute it. Being someone's supervisor means being responsible for that person's performance. You are the boss, and you must act like one.

## Writing Your First Letter of Reference

Another milestone in a newly minted assistant professor's career is the first time a master's student asks you for a letter of recommendation for a doctoral program or when a doctoral student asks you to support her candidacy for a job on the tenure track.[2] That moment is a golden one. Where once you were the supplicant, you have now become the assister of life paths. The task is one few of us are trained for. No tenure-track job description includes "must be a good reference-letter writer." However, such letters, and how you treat the students who ask for them, also contribute toward showing "how much he cares about us."

The initial problem you will confront is how positive to be about the candidate. Academia is suffering from reference overkill. The pressure to be ever more praising has led to widespread discounting of the vague or general letter. Increasingly as well, a premium is put on the quality of the source. Some reference-letter writers are trusted implicitly, but not everybody has such a reputation.

One accomplished professor at a major university, for instance, was regarded as too nice. Any hard-luck student, no matter their competence or achievement, got a glowing, superlative-spattered letter from this fellow. The result was that most people in the field no longer valued his recommendation, regardless of the merits of the student being recommended. You do not want to join the ranks of such "uninfluentials" so early in your career. Remember that some of the professors who get those reference letters or speak to you on the phone as a reference may be the same people who write letters of evaluation for your tenure packet, or even inspect you for an open position if you are switching tenure tracks.

Writing good, honest letters is a win-win consideration for your campaign to create a good reputation for yourself and for the benefit of your students. Furthermore, it is part of the social contract we all sign on to when we seek out a career as an educator.

**Create criteria for accepting recommendation requests.** Because many of us do not think about the issue of reputation early enough in our career, we tend to treat the writing of letters of recommendation as an ad hoc enterprise. Thus we are led into contradictions, contortions, and sometimes embarrassments.

I recall that one of my earliest letters of recommendation was for a student I had serious qualms about supporting to go on to a doctoral program. I felt that he lacked maturity and had failed to show the necessary work ethic. At the time, it never occurred to me that I could turn down a petition, so I wrote a recommendation and tried to put the best face on his qualifications. About a year later, another student with a similar profile asked me for my support in a reference letter. I had grown more wary, however, and turned him down. He was friends with the first student, though, and reasonably asked why I refused him after having accommodated his pal. I had no polite answer. Now I have a checklist that helps me help students and, I hope, keeps my reputation intact.

**Know the student.** Among the items in any checklist should be some quantitative and qualitative judgments of how familiar you are with the work and character of the subject of your letter of recommendation. For example, a political science professor at a regional state university that was well known for feeding undergraduates to major graduate programs developed a similar checklist. Among the sine qua non items to get him to write a letter:

- The student must have taken at least two classes from him and received an A in each.
- The student must have talked with him in office hours extensively.
- The first letter must be requested within two years of matriculation so that he feels he remembers enough about the student.
- The professor must be convinced the graduate program or non-academic employment in question is a good fit.

Perhaps the requirements are strict, but they certainly allow the professor to speak about the student in the letter with authority, and the targets of the letter probably appreciate his thoroughness in vetting those he recommends to them.

**Employ detail and tailoring.** When you are crafting your written recommendation, get into the habit of making it detailed and consistently relevant to the subject.

For example, human beings are storytelling animals, and I try never to offer a recommendation without some anecdote that may illustrate a larger point about the subject's character, teaching skills, research acumen, or collegiality. I once wrote a letter of recommendation for a master's student for a doctoral program in which I recounted how she had volunteered to help edit the papers of several international students who were having trouble with the complicated terminology in our field. I described how she sat down with them, reviewed their work, and made both corrections for basic grammar and suggestions for punching up the prose. I used this description to illustrate her conscientiousness and dedication to pedagogy. Any student worth recommending has some such story that you can recall. Bring it to the fore.

When you have finished your letter, read it over and ask yourself, "Could I have written this about any good student?" Remember reciprocity. Would this be the kind of letter you would want someone to write about you? Woolly and vague letters that sound plug-and-play don't help the applicant, and they make you look like you were lazy or did not care enough to include helpful anecdotes or pertinent factual details.

**Express limitations of view and knowledge.** Almost every recommendation form asks you how long and in what capacity you have known the applicant. Here is where you want to develop another skill set that will apply to the hundreds of recommendation letters to come: caution about your insight. Do not oversell your knowledge of the subject. It is a bit of a stretch, for example, to claim in a reference letter for a doctoral advisee applying for an assistant professor position that "Cersei is a terrific teacher" if you only sat in on one of her classes, she never worked for you as a teaching assistant, you have not reviewed her evaluations, and you never witnessed her engaging undergraduates one-on-one.

To some extent, expressing limited knowledge indemnifies you in case, as unfortunately does happen, someone does not live up to his or her promise. Be clear and unafraid to say, "I can't speak to Cersei's teaching abilities, not having observed them closely enough; however . . ." and then describe those professor-potential qualities with which you are familiar in the candidate. Likewise, you should also describe the relationship qualitatively, in the sense of: have you served as her mentor for career advice as well as research; did you observe her teaching versus, say, only having her as your assistant in support to your own pedagogy?

**Avoid overpraise.** Evaluation forms also ask you to rate qualities of work or character. Most faculty with high reputations for candor and assessment of students never put the top rating across the board. Nobody is that good, and indicating someone is perfect in twelve separate categories makes it look like you did not think before you filled in the box. It is also unhelpful to the candidate (and your standing as a reference) to contribute more cant to the vast heap of over-recommendations, where applicants are all made out to be future Nobel Prize winners, charismatic teachers, and saintly colleagues. In fact, with your first letter of recommendation, you might hurt yourself and come off a bit immature if you get too excited and certainly if you overindulge in the exclamation points! I once did a double-take when, as graduate director, I received a letter of recommendation for a student applying to a doctoral program I supervised that included several sentences typed all in capital letters. The author was an assistant professor, whom I can't blame for being a cheerleader for his students, but he had a bit to learn about the tone of the genre with which he was just beginning to become familiar.

**Disqualify yourself when you aren't qualified.** Sometimes the best service you do a student and yourself is when you do none. Several times during my tenure-track years I felt harried and agreed to write letters of recommendation, and then put them off until the last minute and beyond. I felt guilty, as well I should. Learning to say no when you really, really don't have the time to write a letter of reference is better than accepting the responsibility and then failing to complete it. Still, if you are too busy to write a letter of recommendation for one of your best students then you are plain too busy. Helping students is, after all, our primary job. So weigh the ethical cost of saying no.

There are other times when declining to act as a reference is proper because you are not the right person to help the student. Letters of recommendation are often status-judged—that is, the perception of their value is relative to the rank and CV of the sender. Good letters from assistant professors are valuable for an application to a doctoral program, for example, especially if the writer is a recent graduate who knows the faculty at the target institution well. If your student is applying for a tenure-track job, on the other hand, a strong letter from a high-status senior faculty member might carry greater weight.

In other instances you may be able to write a specialized letter of recommendation. A master's student once asked a physicist to recommend her for a prestigious doctoral program in the sciences. The subfield of the letter writer, however, was completely different from that of the target program, with no connections of faculty or publications. The professor wisely told the student, "You have to find someone who is more of a peer to speak for your potential for research in that area. I can speak to your work habits; I'll write only about them."

Sometimes, there are even political reasons to bow out of writing a letter. One senior professor declined to serve as a reference for a student because a member of the search committee for the job in question and she had some strong differences of opinion on a research area. Unfortunately, they had a high degree of antagonism as well, even having gotten into verbal tussles at conferences. Both of them, as professionals, should have attempted to disregard personal feelings in the service of a truly gifted student, but in academia the political, the professional, and the personal often interfere with one another. The would-be reference believed it was safer to abstain from providing the recommendation.

In sum, when you recommend someone, the person stands for you, and if you really want to help him, you should be as thoughtful and caring about the style, form, and content of the recommendation as you would want someone to be about a reference for yourself.

## Showing You Care about Them: Why?

Teachers have ruminated over the best way to teach since there was an activity that passed for teaching. I imagine 12,000 years ago a senior Paleolithic pedagogue tried to instruct a young pupil on the art and science of the big-game hunt by pointing out pertinent features of a mammoth on a cave painting: the first visually illustrated textbook. And when the student looked both bored and bewildered, the teacher thought, "I'm not getting through to this guy. Is it me or him?"

Likewise, the modern higher educator often scans the faces in the lecture hall or lab and wonders, "Are they learning?" For the assistant professor or even the midcareer associate, the question is one whose answer affects both success in the classroom and career prospects. The weight of teaching in determining P&T can be either modest or all-important, depending on where you work. Fortunately, voluminous research on classroom deportment, styles, and method—via publications, consultations with master-teachers in your discipline, and your school's teaching improvement center—is available for the instructor who wants to become a better teacher.

There are, however, parts of the teaching experience that, although less thoroughly studied, are crucial not only to being a good teacher and being recognized as such by students and peers but also to enhancing the satisfaction (and yes, fun!) of being a college educator today. This chapter on student relations concludes with a discussion of two ways to care about students and *show* how much you care about students. I will focus on two neglected physical dimensions of your work: comments on papers and office hours. Both have considerable people, politics, and personal causes and consequences.

## Showing You Care about Them: How
## (Through Comments on Papers)

One task is considered by some to be one of the great drudgeries of our business, but by others the most expressive art form of the teacher. It is the seemingly prosaic but actually quite vital writing of comments on student papers.

In the pre-FERPA (Family Educational Rights and Privacy Act) days, faculty left giant boxes of marked final essays outside their doors in December only to find that well into the spring term few students had retrieved theirs. Nowadays, the papers wait in cabinets, their comments unread by students who have not come by to pick them up. Sometimes we return papers to students, by hand or electronically, and vainly hope that the young ones will gain in wisdom by reading our insights. Some assert that this is the inevitable fate of the final essay or term paper. Today's criticism-averse students try to avoid hearing that anything is wrong with their work. And as for comments on papers written during the school year that we return in class and expect the students to absorb? Alas, who reads them?

I contributed to a book that sums up some of the existing knowledge of educators.[3] Most of the other teachers who wrote the essays were instructors of English composition, but we all shared the concern that a fundamental principle of teaching is that the student should have the opportunity to hear what you have to say about their work. More than that, we live in a world where professional critiques of work are rare. Once upon a time, if you submitted a novel to an agent, or a story to a magazine, you would get back some detailed comments, even in the case of rejection. These days, the form letter or e-mail is ubiquitous. Higher education is the last place you can get a credentialed expert who cares about you and your work to respond to you regularly and reliably. Students *should* treasure such an opportunity.

The issue is also one that should concern college teachers for many reasons beyond the most important: that students should get a good learning experience in the classroom. Comments are a P&T issue.

First, the sheer time expended on writing comments demands that they have some purpose besides hearing oneself scribble or type. In addition, while students judge teachers on many criteria, most evaluation forms have some version of assessments like "the teacher made clear to me her/his expectations" and "the teacher cared about my progress in the class."

Also, you will not be a good teacher (or rated as such) if you don't enjoy being a good teacher. Feeling that the students listen to you and respect your advice bolsters the satisfaction of the job—and that helps your career ascent as well.

On the actual writing of commentary, here are some basic rules:

- Write clearly. Bad handwriting in your comments tells students that you don't care enough to be unambiguously understood. (The problem is solved, of course, if you respond to online or e-papers via typed comments.)
- Write to be read. Explain your views as if the student were there sitting next to you, intently listening.
- Don't just flag the problems; offer solutions.
- Tie in comments to points made in class. Students often don't see links between reading, class lectures and discussions, and the term paper.
- Be specific. The term paper comment is a not a genre that calls for rambling and stumbling. Tell students exactly what you want them to do or change.
- Be brief. The longer the comment, the less it is likely to be read.
- Restrain bitterness or sarcasm. Never succumb to the temptation to mock student ignorance, sloth, and folly. Think of ways to make your point, even about egregious errors, without humiliating or belittling the 18-year-old.

All the above advice is helpful if, and only if, you can get a student to read the comments. Here is where tenure-trekking academics can heighten both the satisfaction of teaching (for themselves) and the utility of learning for their charges. *Treat the scrutiny and response to comments as part of the "live" classroom experience.* Consider the old method: you hand out papers in class, make some general statement, invite the students to drop by the office to talk about their grades, and then you move on to another topic. That is a system designed for failure.

Instead, make time and space for talking about your reactions to papers. In class you can show comments that you made (while providing the individual student anonymity); better yet, you can display common comments from the last semester's papers *before* students write a similar paper in the current class. (More and more faculty are using social media, like blogs, to feature posts and comments.) You can offer students an incentive to read your comments by creating assignments where they must respond within a newer version of a paper. For the final paper, think about having it due earlier than the end of the semester and direct students to come talk to you about it as their true exit assignment.

Next, employ preemptive auto-commentary. Ask students to attach to their paper their own critiques of it. Reward them with points for the incisiveness of their self-appraisal. The purposes of this exercise are (a) to get students to appreciate that criticism is not necessarily "negative" or a form of personal attack but should have improvement as its goal and (b) to demonstrate that those who can edit themselves are more likely to do better in school and in jobs.

All such strategies assist in redirecting student focus from the single number or letter grade, or at least help students place that mark in the wider context of their actual performance. Moreover, engaging in face time in the classroom or in the office to talk about *how* you graded a paper makes a stronger case to students that the process is not arbitrary. In other words, train students to think of your comments as part of the required texts for the course. You will find that if you can generate post-paper interactions, you will become a better teacher, students will learn more, and you will improve in the "cares about my progress" and "helps me" categories on the evaluation—and, with any luck, in the students' hearts and minds as well.

It can work. A friend who teaches creative writing shared a note from a student that he received at the end of the semester. It said, "Thank you for caring enough to correct me."

So write comments to be read, and design ways to ensure that your students read them. The outcome will be better for all involved, and you will find your tenure-track satisfactions growing.

## Showing You Care about Them: How (Through Office Hours)

Everyone in higher education has a favorite teaching venue. Some of us like the small seminar, or a laboratory section, or the lecture hall, or even distance learning. I have discovered both pleasures and penances in each type of class setting, but the one that most appeals to me, because of its focus on interactive, face-to-face learning, is the office tête-à-tête. In fact, I've often thought that the office hour is where the modern higher education instructor best approximates what it must have been like for Plato and Socrates to philosophize with their students in the first olive grove of academia.

Office hours also matter because there is an irretrievability factor with students and teaching. If you submit an article to a journal and it is turned down, the situation, unless you're up against the final gong of the tenure clock, is salvageable. You can rewrite it and resubmit it to another journal. Once you've made mistakes in the classroom, however—had a poor and frustrating teaching experience and been zapped by low evaluations—the damage is final. A black cloud resides in your memory and a black spot in your record for the P&T committee, the dean, and the outside evaluators.

Productive office meetings with students can be a basis for a successful classroom.[4] It is there that you can show that "the instructor cared about me and my learning experience." You get to sit down and focus individually on one student or small groups of students. You can take a break to check something on the Web or pull a book off the shelf for reference. You can satisfy the students' intellectual curiosity better than in the preprogrammed class setting.

All that is possible only if students show up. Office hours should become a formal part of your teaching, and not an unassigned afterthought. Likewise, the office hour is a crucial interchange. Yes, for huge lecture classes it is almost impossible to meet everyone in person. But for all classes, you should find a way to assign or entice each student to see you at least once per term.

If you teach at a community college or a small liberal arts college, there are the official office hours and the unofficial ones—what you have posted versus the longer times students (and administrators) expect you be around for student drop-ins. On commuter campuses, the culture may be more oriented toward longer office availability. But assistant professors at research universities have no obligation to sit at their desks from 8 to 5 waiting for somebody to drop by to talk to them.

That doesn't mean, however, that you should not keep the regular office-hour and by-appointment commitments. The surest way to communicate to students that you don't care about them is to cancel your office hours frequently or show up late. If you have to step out of the office, leave a note with your exact return time. If you go out for longer than ten minutes, extend your office hours accordingly.

Be there in mind and spirit as well as in body. Don't start some complicated creative task. Engage only in activities that are easy to drop when a student appears at the door.[5]

The research shows students are timid about "bothering" you unless there is an urgent matter, and even then they may see you as forbidding.[6] That's why your space must be as welcoming as your demeanor. Take the case of one young mass communications scholar. When he first started teaching, he practiced, apparently wholly unconsciously, what might be best described as a fascist aesthetic of furniture–human interface. He placed his big, heavy desk in the middle of the room facing the door with chairs for students in front of it. His computer's bulging monitor was turned toward him. A student talking to him, thus, was confronted by metal, wood, and plastic that occluded vision of the teacher. Worse, even during office hours he kept his door open only a crack and his lights dimmed. The message: I don't have time to or interest in helping you.

Since then he has tried to make his office exude a conference format and welcoming atmosphere. His desk is against the wall, out of the way. He keeps a circular table in the center of the room where he can sit to review papers and materials, and look at laptop screens—that is, where he and his students can interact as *humans*. His lights are bright, the door is open. The message: Welcome! I have time for and interest in helping you.

Which brings up the issue of timing. When I myself was a new assistant professor, I set office hour slots of two hours each at the same times on a Monday and a Wednesday. But few students came to see me. I chalked it up to the usual undergraduate lack of motivation to talk to the professor unless it was just before or after an exam. Our kind and wise undergraduate counselor, however, pointed out to me that the time slot that I picked was when many students had basic classes. Furthermore, it was extremely likely that anyone who was in a Monday class at one time slot would also be in the same class on Wednesday. I switched (and staggered) my times to better accommodate student schedules. I also learned to find creative ways to meet students by appointment.

Giving students time and attention in your office does not mean forgetting all the rules of time management. Let's say that it's the week after you've returned a midterm paper and seven or eight students show up to talk to you at the start of office hours. But the first in line has lots of issues and the clock ticks; you sense the rumblings of discontent outside the door. Some of them even leave in frustration. Do you cut the present student short or keep going?

A sober analysis begins with the observation that you didn't plan the hours correctly. If you anticipate a rush, put up a schedule on the door letting students book certain blocks of time—say, twenty minutes each—so they don't have to wait. If one student meeting starts to go long, set up another appointment to continue.

The nature of office hours conversation is another area that requires forethought. Some students want to get their business done and go; others may have larger queries, from career choices to the meaning of life. One young lady stopped by my office and, with a few minutes left in office hours after a truly long and tiring day, asked me plaintively, "Do you think I should marry my boyfriend and work at the mall, or become an anthropologist?"

How much you want to talk to students about personal issues is your own call, but you should be keenly aware of your institution's rules about what student problems need to (or legally *must*) be referred to the counseling office or some other campus student service. Professors can offer career advice but should stay away from lifestyle and love guru-ship, both because we are not qualified for that kind of counseling and because it is professionally inappropriate.

The technology issue is also relevant. In an age of Twittering and text messaging, I have wondered whether students will eventually junk the office hour. I believe and hope not, and in fact I argue that academics should be evangelistic for face-to-face contact with students outside of lectures. Yes, online and distance learning can work, but if students are in a setting where there is an actual classroom, the office is a necessary extension of it. No matter how online or wireless our students are, they will, if coaxed, find value in face-to-face mentoring. Again, if they feel you care about them, they will return the favor.

That point sums up the ethos of this chapter. Almost every tenure track has some expectation of decent or excellent performance in teaching. But good pedagogy is not just about getting marks on a 1-to-5 scale and attracting comments like, "She was real neat." It's about finding a way to find happiness in the core activity of being someone who professes for a living. That contentment will reflect well in your student evaluations, peer mentoring, and any other quantitative and qualitative measures of effective teaching in your classes. It also will give sustenance to your spirit, allowing you to succeed in the other necessary components of P&T.

# CHAPTER 6

# Steps to Tenure and Promotion
# and Beyond

❋

Sometimes people get tenure and promotion through one significant event: a researcher at a major state school having won a prestigious award in her field, for instance, or a tenure tracker at a tiny religious college becoming best friends with the university president. But generally, P&T, and indeed career success in academia, is the outcome of a confluence of many actions, decisions, ideas, circumstances, and, of course, the vagaries of three-P. While the array of factors can be complicated, even confusing, most people agree that at least some kind of struggle is involved that leaves the participant nearly exhausted and often frazzled by the time she reaches the goal.

Unfortunately, sometimes people progress and prosper through their graduate programs, job search, and tenure track, and then blow it by some last gasp of unmindfulness, incompetence, or poor decision making. Take a young social scientist at a research university who had been publishing quite well for three or four years and then committed to a book project that she hoped and expected would be completed in time to be counted toward P&T. But she violated nearly all the rules of time management and good stewardship of resources and assistants; growing crabbier at the prospect of failure, she started alienating her colleagues and her students as well. She was voted down for tenure despite what everyone lamented was her original promising start. Perhaps at a university that had not put a huge emphasis on steady research productivity, as hers did, her early and middle successes would have counted enough. But she was a classic case of what Lincoln called the ability of some to "snatch defeat from the jaws of victory."

Hence this chapter. Here I try to review some critical bureaucratic as well as political and human elements of the final stages of the tenure process. I also comment on scenarios of folly and success, what to do if you are denied tenure, and why it isn't the end of the world. And I provide some parting thoughts on how to enjoy, if briefly, the awarding of tenure more than most of us do and then think about the much longer career that is to come.

## Presenting Your Tenure File

Sometimes tenure trackers forget that it's not just *you* going up for P&T but also a bundle of materials associated with your name: the tenure packet, which, as of this writing in 2010, is still mostly paper. Your packet will be inspected by your departmental P&T committee, the head of your unit, a set of outside reviewers, a university-level P&T committee (also possibly a college or division-level committee if your unit is a department within such a larger organization), and then a high-level university administrator such as the provost. In almost no case will you be there personally to answer questions, explain items, or influence perceptions. Your packet must speak for itself and argue for you.

Of course, in such an important set of documents, substance trumps style. But appearances matter, too, and how much they matter can depend on the substance. Say you're applying for P&T in history, and the key component of your packet is a published book by a major university press that has won a significant national award and laudatory reviews in top journals. Odds are that you will get a favorable recommendation from an outside reviewer even if the copy you submitted within the packet is weather-stained and dog-eared. Alternately, if you are a psychologist and have not published the requisite number of articles in the right journals, an aesthetically pleasing and impeccably organized packet will do you no good. In one case at a community college, the full-color, laser-printed pie charts that dazzlingly displayed the candidate's peer and student evaluations could not obscure the fact that the ratings were universally low.

Nevertheless, the *presentation* of the tenure file—the arrangement of materials, and the choices about which items to include and the best way to exhibit them—is a significant factor in how they are evaluated, especially by external actors: university-level committees and outside reviewers. Even if people who give up their time to review your case strive to be fair and candid, they can't help but be negatively influenced by a file that is poorly laid out, with relevant documents missing, and no context provided for teaching-evaluation scores or journal-acceptance rates.

So form does count. Some basic principles hold for the construction and arrangement of any P&T file.

**If possible, check your file before it is sent out to reviewers.** One of the great conundrums of tenure-packet presentation is that often you are at the mercy of others. Stories abound of assistant professors going up for tenure and learning later that their neatly styled and organized portfolio was "helpfully" rearranged by well-meaning but incompetent staff members or senior professors, or worse, by villains who wanted to make the candidate look bad. One assistant professor recounted that she was so distrustful of the packet-assembling skills of the head of the P&T committee that she appealed to her dean to be allowed to put it together on her own. Institutional rules and traditions vary, but you are primarily responsible for knowing what is required and assembling your tenure file. Outside evaluators and committees will assume that any problems are your fault, even if they are not.

**Begin organizing your tenure file in your first year on the tenure track.** We all need a periodic curriculum vitae (CV) check. Circulate your vita to respected mentors in your home department and in your field, and ask for suggestions. Establish a fixed layout for your CV, and train yourself to update it regularly. Some people put a reminder on their calendar to "update CV" on the first day of every month. One school in which I taught had a Monday Memo with faculty news; I routinely took whatever information I submitted to that newsletter and put it on my CV. Create a way to keep track of your achievements and activities in research, teaching, and service but with this caveat: your institution will have its own format for tenure materials. You will need to make sure your organizational system is in compliance. You must know the P&T rules and procedures and adhere to them.

**Follow your format and include the correct materials.** The most attractive tenure packets consist of documents organized into separate sections—book chapters, journal articles, teaching documents, service documents. Each grouping of information should have a labeled tab to make it easy to spot, and a differently colored title page. Failure to label can confuse the intended audience. I was surprised to see a book manuscript in one tenure packet. The CV and cover letter gave no indication that the pages were either under submission or under contract. In short, the manuscript did not count for P&T, so why was it included? I have also seen articles that were published before the candidate's tenure clock began; these were not relevant to the evaluation under the institution's rules—or were they? I was not told what counted. Worse is missing important documents altogether; the message sent is "I don't care."

**Give some context, including background information and standards.** The "who did what" of the tenure packet is a crucial element to help reviewers judge you, especially when the institution's P&T guidelines include specific standards, like number of articles published in major journals. How can a reviewer evaluate an article's weight toward your promotion if you are the third and final author and you don't explain your contribution to the effort? For service activities, for example, it helps to know what, specifically, your five years on the graduate-awards committee entailed. Keep your contextual annotations as brief as possible so that you don't overwhelm reviewers with details. In general, however, it is better to overexplain than to underexplain.

You do have the right to ask your department, tactfully, how the criteria will be described or presented to outside reviewers. A good cover letter delineates the standards and focus of the review, but these vary by institution and program. For example, a letter might instruct, "Please let us know if this candidate would get promotion and tenure at your institution," or, "Please assess our candidate by the attached university promotion and tenure criteria," or (very common), "We do not ask you to determine whether the candidate deserves tenure but rather to assess his scholarship; other reviewers will address his teaching and service."

**Don't spin or puff up your record.** Don't undersell or oversell. Do not try to elevate a tiny press or an unknown journal into the ranks of the most prestigious. The evaluators in your field will know. It is likely worth noting any special circumstances to a very low teaching evaluation you received in a particular course, such as its difficulty or unpopularity with students, but don't mislead. Reliable third-party sources are what reviewers will expect: the acceptance rates of journals, the comparative scores of evaluations in a course, even a notation in your file about how a particular class is viewed as extremely challenging to instructors by other faculty. A colleague said she once reviewed a P&T packet in which "everything that was listed as 'major' was objectively 'minor.'" You will not spin your way to P&T. In fact, you will hurt your case if the reviewers sense you are trying to deceive them or play a shell game with information.

The content of a tenure packet is undoubtedly more important than its presentation. But, as in many other aspects of life and labor, professionalism in packaging and design counts. The best thing you can do for your tenure packet is to make it as impressive in clarity and organization as in substance.

## Selecting Outside Evaluators

Of all the service duties of the modern tenured academic, acting as an outside reviewer for P&T is the most challenging because we know what is at stake. Reviewers evaluate candidates about whose work they may know quite a lot (and thus have preexisting prejudices about their qualifications) or nothing at all except the records presented in the tenure dossier. Some institutions will seek out reviewers who do not know you personally at all, but this is an increasingly difficult task among specialized subfields, where the cohort is small. From the candidate's point of view, while you can't control what your outside reviewers say about you, you do have some influence on who gets asked to evaluate you and who doesn't. And there are steps you can take to increase the odds for a fair review. The selection of outside evaluators varies from place to place but has some common elements. Typically, a tenure candidate is required to submit a list of names of potential reviewers. The department chair, faculty, and/or members of the internal tenure committee also submit a list. The candidate and department chair meet to discuss and arrive at some agreed-on names. In other cases, the chair of the department and the head of the P&T committee will pool the nominations and derive a master target list. Almost always, at least some of the names that you, the candidate, pick will end up being reviewers of your P&T file.

There are standard qualifications and disqualifications for the selections: your dissertation adviser and publication coauthors can't evaluate your tenure case. Evaluators must be tenured. If you're an associate professor seeking promotion, your reviewers usually must be full professors. Typically, institutions have stipulations that reviewers come from "peer" colleges and universities.

However chosen, outside reviewers can be a critical influence and a crucial voice in the P&T process. It is quite possible, for example, that a tenure candidate is the sole researcher and teacher in a particular subfield in the department. In that case, the local P&T committee and/or faculty should seek external "peer elders" in the same subfield who can offer an expert perspective.

So what factors should you consider as you put together your part of the list of outside reviewers?

**Network forward.** You shouldn't be so careerist as to identify outside reviewers on your first day on the tenure track and start bombarding them with compliments. But you should begin building a reputation so that other scholars in your field and subfield have heard good things about you, read your work, or heard you give papers at conferences. (In the chapter on the doctoral years, I recommended starting to network then.) Certainly, getting published and frequently cited in journals or at conferences is vital for the research scholar. The tenure tracker at a community college or a small liberal arts institution may contribute to publications on teaching or field-wide newsletters or Web sites. Involvement in national organizations in your discipline is another way to become known and, you hope, renowned. As a scholar, you should always expand the number of your contacts. If you read a great paper in a journal, drop the author a note of appreciation and ask some follow-up questions. Consulting a more experienced colleague at another college about syllabus design also adds new contacts and heightens your reputation. This is not buttering up; it's self-improvement. We often say that scholarship is created by standing on the shoulders of those who have researched before us; why not talk to those same giants as well?

**Be honest in your nominations.** Populate your list with people whom it makes sense to include. If, for instance, all five of your nominated reviewers are outside of your subfield, the tenure committee will suspect, with reason, that (a) you are afraid of being judged by true "peers," or (b) your choices are pals and would not be honest jurors. Your department has some veto power regarding names of potential reviewers. So you will need to explain your selections to the departmental committee or the chair. What is your relationship, if any, with the nominees? What are their credentials? What aspects of your portfolio can they best speak to? Now is the time for full disclosure. To conceal that you are working on a paper with one of the reviewers on your list or to inflate their status in the field is unethical and will be detected. Remember that the committee will ask outside reviewers to provide their CVs and to describe their relationship with you.

**Choose people with the best possible credentials.** You don't have to list five Nobel laureates as your outside reviewers. Just make sure their CVs demonstrate that they are significant in your field or subfield, based on published scholarship and/or leadership. The reputation and affiliations of your outside evaluators will, of course, affect how much weight their opinion carries with your department, top administrators, and campus-wide tenure committees. It is tempting to lowball the reviewer standard—that is, to pick people who just meet the minimum qualifications for an outside evaluator, the idea being that they will be more likely to ladle out praise than would the superstar senior scholar. The problem with that strategy is that it is disingenuous and transparent.

**Choose people who understand your work.** Prestige is fine, but an insightful and competent evaluation of a tenure packet is complicated and demanding. One reviewer might overlook something in facing a mass of materials, especially if he is not familiar with its significance. Suggest evaluators who understand your area of specialization, including its jargon and measures of achievement.

For example, a mass communications social scientist who often serves as a reviewer in his field taught the "101" introductory course when he was an assistant professor himself. When he evaluates tenure candidates who have taught a lot of introductory-level courses, he has a good deal of background with which to assess their student-evaluation scores, syllabi, classroom materials, and teaching philosophy. At the same time, one of his prime areas of research is visual communication, so he is familiar with the top journals and the most-cited scholars in that subfield. His expertise does not mean that his evaluations will be better or fairer than those of a reviewer who has never taught 101 courses or published in visual communication, but his judgment will be more tied to similar experiences of the candidate, which cannot be a bad thing.

**Know when to go negative.** The nomination game has one thorny aspect. At many institutions, you are allowed to specify people you do *not* want as your outside reviewers. The reasons vary as much as the human condition. An assistant professor requested a potential evaluator not be used because "she is stalking me since we made out at a conference." (He allegedly said this in conversation, not in a note to the dean.)

Offer only minimal explanation when you name those you hope to omit from the reviewers' list. Also, once you go beyond two or three names, committee members may wonder how many enemies you have made in your (as yet) short career. As a tenure candidate, you have to trust that most reviewers take the responsibility of writing an external review seriously.

## Surviving the Checkback

For six years, as an assistant professor, the primary focus of your career planning and angst has been tenure. Now comes that postpartum moment when you are notified that your complete packet, including the outside letters of evaluation, has been sent up to the university-wide P&T committee, and then on to senior administrators. Finally, there is nothing left for you to print out, file, or sign. Sure, you are concerned about the outcome, but you're relieved that the long quest is about to end, for better or worse. There is one last step, however, in the process for which you need to muster all of your mental wiles, bureaucratic skills, and three-P sensitivity—the "checkback," and it can pose the ultimate hurdle, threat, or opportunity.

The checkback is a request for more information about your case. It can come from a college P&T committee, from a university-wide committee (most commonly), or from the senior administration. They bring fresh eyes and minds to your tenure file and may see defects or omissions that your departmental colleagues and even your outside evaluators did not notice. It can be a simple matter of providing a minor piece of information that is somehow missing. Or perhaps you have to clarify the acceptance rate of a journal in which you published. You may be asked a wide-ranging series of questions that require a detailed (but speedy) response. Or the checkback may be so extensive that you would be wise to freeze the tenure process and not go through with it at all. (That option will be discussed later in this chapter.)

The rules of the checkback vary. Sometimes the tenure candidate is asked to answer questions directly. Alternately, the request may be sent to a candidate's department chair or the head of the departmental P&T committee, with the candidate being informed of the contents but not directly involved. Almost always the turnaround time for a response is short—weeks, or even days.

For the most part, the checkback is a normal part of the process and not necessarily a sign of trouble. But it is serious business. Tone, style, content, and even timing are crucial. Whether you draft the reply or someone else does it on your behalf, you need to be prepared, bureaucratically and cognitively.

**Be on call.** The world is run, it is often said, by people who show up. Don't be marked "absent" at your checkback. If at all possible, find out if there are set times and dates during which checkbacks are most likely to be sent out. Be around and available then. Of course, in this age of iPhone and voicemail, you don't have to be constantly in your office, awaiting word from on high. But avoid the fate of the assistant professor who, away on a trip when a checkback came, failed to retrieve his phone messages for days. You don't have unlimited time to respond to the checkback, and, indeed, the longer it takes to craft a response, the more it implies that you were either unprepared for the question or are spinning your wheels to concoct an answer.

**Plan ahead.** You should have all your P&T documents organized and available for immediate consultation when the call comes. Keep a complete copy of your file—perhaps at home in case the query shows up in e-mail at 4:59 p.m. on a Friday.

Sometimes you may have a hint of problematic issues. One assistant professor in the sciences at a small college got contradictory advice about whether to include teaching scores from a semester-long stint as a visiting scholar in his tenure packet. The consensus of his departmental mentors was that the material was not required. Sure enough, the checkback came with a request for that very information.

Other times you are well aware of the points of debate, controversy, or even deficiency in your case. I've heard from several correspondents who received tenure after a contentious process; all of them said they knew exactly what was going to cause trouble. One was aware that he had several years of poor teaching evaluations because of illness, and the checkback in his case focused on those scores. He had already prepared a written explanation, which evidently satisfied everyone because he was awarded tenure.

**Follow procedure.** The checkback is one bureaucratic procedure for which you must, at all costs, follow protocol to the letter. Make sure you know your institution's P&T guidelines; consult them again and seek clarification from your mentors or from department leaders. You should have taken notes at meetings about your case and discussed how to respond to checkbacks; save all e-mail exchanges. Your best source of information regarding a checkback might be a friendly senior professor who has had long experience on the university's tenure committee. A checkback is an attempt to fill in a missing hole; make sure you are prepared to plug it with a peg of the correct size, dimension, and color.

**Answer the questions comprehensively and concisely.** If the checkback is simply a document request, such as for a certain year's teaching evaluations or a published journal article, your task is rather straightforward. Things get dangerous when the question is more complicated and requires a written response. Suddenly, you are crafting an essay of sorts in a genre with which most of us have no practice. Say the checkback concerns your lower-than-average teaching evaluations. Perhaps you can mobilize statistics to show your teaching scores have risen steadily and that outlying lower scores were in the earliest years on the tenure track when you were just getting the hang of teaching some difficult courses. While you should write a narrative explanation, it also might be useful to provide a visual chart. Then schedule a meeting with the people in your department who are in charge of your case, and make sure they understand and approve of your answer (assuming you feel they are on your side).

**Be factual, not defensive.** A checkback is not a personal attack nor an invitation to vigorous argument. You might be offended by a question about something of which you are particularly proud—for instance, doubts about a certain publication or service work you performed for the university. But even if your feelings are hurt, or you sense that people are indeed out to get you—which is always a possibility—you must be businesslike and even-toned in your response. Avoid incendiary words or phrases.

Sabotage of a tenure case by someone on an internal tenure committee is rare, but it happens. An arts scholar at a regional state university alleged that members of the departmental committee had strongly opposed his going up early for tenure. "They tried to get tricky," he said, "and hide or ignore external peer reviews, make up numbers, and state that the file was missing complete documentation." He uncovered the iniquities during the checkback phase. After much paper shuffling and detective work, he was able to make his case to the top administration and the university P&T committee, and was awarded tenure despite the opposition.

Sometimes, because of the huge workload of tenure committees and their unfamiliarity with your discipline, items and issues that are straightforward to you might need further explanation to them. A tenure tracker at a community college was irritated by his checkback because a major item said to be missing from his file was, in fact, included. His reply to the committee was curt. Fortunately, his department chair wisely rewrote his response in polite and informational terms. The candidate got tenure and now admits that nothing would have been gained by putting his ire into print. The same point applies to humor. Academia needs more levity, but making sarcastic, ironic, or sardonic remarks in a checkback response will likely mean the joke is on you.

**Explain insider items for outsiders.** Sometimes a checkback arises from a misunderstanding or mistranslation across fields or disciplines. Or a committee might seek clarifications of matters that are obvious to someone in your field but require explanation for outsiders. Remember, the people on the campus-wide tenure committee are seasoned faculty members who face one of the heaviest service tasks in academia. If you are, say, a violinist, you might have a committee of physicists, sociologists, and librarians trying to decipher your achievements, while the ultimate arbiter, the provost, is an archaeologist.

For example, one veteran committee member described getting a tenure file that said the candidate was primary author on most of his published research. Yet several committee members noted that he was listed last in every multiple-authored paper. A checkback was necessary to learn that, in the candidate's discipline, authorship was always assigned alphabetically, no matter what the contribution of effort. In general, if your case is less than clear-cut at the department level, with a split vote or outside letters of support that disagree on your qualifications, small items may count for much. Therefore, when crafting your response or providing information to those who review your record, make sure the information is user-friendly—that is, decipherable to those outside your specialization. Refrain from using jargon, acronyms, or abbreviations.

All the above conditions and considerations assume that the checkback is a routine one of minor or moderate consequence. In some cases, however, the checkback is one of a series of clanging bells that your tenure application is in deep trouble. At that point you will need to make the toughest choice of your academic career in an attempt to save it: you may have to withdraw your tenure bid and give up hope of tenure at your present institution.

## A Final Option: Withdrawing Your Tenure Case

The awarding of tenure is not analogous to winning the lottery or becoming an NBA star. It is in the interests of colleges and universities to hire people who are likely to get tenure and to nurture them to do so. At the University of Iowa, where I teach, the overall tenure rate is 90 percent. We boast of that figure not as signifying a lack of selectivity or a prevalence of lower standards, but as indicating a culture and a bureaucratic and financial support system at the university that propels tenure trackers to success.

But tenure denial is a reality, and *Promotion and Tenure Confidential* does not ignore threats or grim scenarios. So we must look at the ramifications and the recovery strategies to the ultimate challenge of the tenure track: being denied tenure.

At most institutions, ill-fated candidates are made aware through a variety of channels that their tenure bids are on shaky ground. You will certainly learn, for example, if the departmental vote went against you, or if your chair opposes your bid; you hope you will know if your outside letters are tepid or negative. Your chair may simply tell you that your case will not be sent up.

But as mentioned previously, you might also become aware of problems during the checkback which, at that point, can be a late-in-the-game vehicle for either delivering or reinforcing the message that doom is nigh. You now have to make a tough choice. You can go through with the process and probably lose, or you can withdraw your tenure bid.

Why would you want to pull out at the last minute after long, hard years of work, and so close to the prize? Although being denied tenure is not the end of your academic career, it is a tremendous psychological blow and a bureaucratic burden to those who suffer it. The external political complications are worth exploring if you are to appreciate that it is better to sidestep tenure denial.

In some universities and departments, and even in entire disciplines, tenure denial is a permanent black mark against your future hiring. I know of a number of instances in the humanities, arts, and sciences in which candidates were considered good prospects until the hiring committee learned that they had been denied tenure elsewhere. A young assistant professor of English at a research university was the top candidate for a new job until the department discovered that he had just been denied tenure. Note that in his case, as in others, he probably would have gotten the job if he had frozen the tenure process and never received an *official* rejection.

Tenure denial is never a positive addition to a CV, but it conversely can be minimally damaging—for example, being denied tenure by an institution that is viewed as superior and highly choosy. A well-known stream of people who did not achieve tenure at Ivy League universities have found great, prestigious jobs at major state institutions. Likewise, someone may be denied tenure at a department with a reputation as a snake pit of infighting, so people discount the candidate's "failure" as stemming from a dysfunctional environment.

Still, there is no need to claw to the bitter end if you are afforded the opportunity to withdraw.

Let's say your chair tells you, "Word has come from the provost's office that you're probably not going to get tenure." In the year you go up for tenure, it's smart to apply for other positions so that, if the worst happens, you have a back-up opportunity. If you do, it is even more imperative that you withdraw your tenure bid before the denial becomes official. You can simply take another job, and your record will be completely clean.

If, however, you are denied tenure and have no other prospects, you can appeal through the university or the courts. In both cases, you risk wasting time and money and getting nothing in return. Whatever the merits of your appeal or complaint, by making trouble you will get a reputation in academia for being trouble, and nobody likes to hire trouble.

So another argument for withdrawing your tenure bid if it seems nonviable is that doing so may buy you some goodwill. An assistant professor at a small liberal arts college stopped his tenure bid after he got the message that the administration was going to side with a faction of professors that opposed his candidacy. Once he withdrew, he was surprised to find that "everybody started being nice." His enemies were relieved to discover that he would not put up a fight, and they were smart enough to realize that it was in their interest to help him exit with dignity. He was then able to go on the job market with supportive internal advocates and references. He nabbed another job, in a happier environment, and he credits not making a stink and not getting tainted by a tenure denial as among the reasons for his hiring.

If an escape clause will leave your record intact, why is it, then, that people don't take advantage of it more often?

One reason is that there is a winnowing process before candidates go up for tenure. Conscientious department chairs and senior professors use the third-year review (or annual reviews) to hint (or state outright) that a faculty member should try to find another job.

Another factor is that some whose tenure cases are dicey stick it out anyway and win. If you have strong departmental support, or can document serious procedural errors, victory and vindication are certainly possible. People do overcome internal opposition to win tenure.

But what if all the odds (and odds-makers) are against you? Human nature also dictates that people will obstinately fight on, even when every sign and portent indicates that they will be denied tenure. Over the years, I have heard many variations of the following statement: "I knew I was going to be turned down. There was no way that anybody in the department or upper administration would stick up for me. But I had to finish it."

The shock and dismay of all one's hard work seemingly being for nothing is too much for people of both strong and weak will. As one put it, "I'd rather die with my boots on."

If that's your attitude—that P&T is a metaphysical statement of your worth—practical career advice becomes inconsequential. But if you are thinking about your next move, the option to withdraw your P&T bid is still a viable one. Before you ride off to martyred glory, consider the good sense of living to fight another day.

## You Didn't Get Tenure: What Now?

Tenure denial happens. If you have been denied tenure, you need to allow yourself a brief period for mourning, self-pity, anger, blame-gaming, and recrimination. All of those reactions are justified at this time, although none are ultimately practical. So spend a weekend stewing, away from friends and family. Smash a cheap dish. Watch the entire run of HBO's *The Sopranos*. Then return clearheaded, with a plan.

Before you abandon academia to take up the livery trade, a clerkship at a used-book store, or some industry job, consider your alternatives and your real strengths and weaknesses.

**Taking stock.** To begin, assess what happened—but try to remove your ego from the investigation. Was the denial of tenure a surprise to you? Were you under the impression that you had fulfilled the requirements, and then some, of your department and university? Objectivity, always elusive in self-inspection, is even more difficult here, but your future depends on it, so some trusted outside friends may be of help in that analysis as well.

I once talked to a job applicant who, denied tenure by his institution, offered the equivalent of a baseball fan's "We wuz robbed" lament. But when I looked up the tenure standards of his university and compared them to his CV, it was clear that he had, on paper—which is all that should really count—underperformed markedly. So although he may have been denied tenure for a host of other reasons, including the plotting of nefarious enemies, surely his lack of publications and low teaching evaluations left him vulnerable. And I told him just that. His reaction was revealing: "But I *deserved* tenure."

It was clear that his definition of an inalienable right to tenure was different from mine and that of his fellow faculty members. More importantly, his bitterness was dysfunctional: his record was sufficient to get tenure at other kinds of colleges, but he did not work at those, and notably he was still not applying for jobs at those.

Your diagnosis leads to another crucial decision. All colleges and universities have internal appeals processes. Now is the time to read those protocols, procedures, and rules carefully, and even consult with trusted mentors.

The choice as to whether you should appeal your tenure denial depends on too many variables to render a universal verdict here, but certainly the number and rank of people supporting your appeal matter. Because many faculty votes are secret—and only revealed by a lawsuit—figuring out how much support you have is more difficult than it sounds.

A humanities scholar who did get tenure noted that the vote was many-to-one in favor but that every faculty member had assured him, "You got my vote." He still doesn't know which colleague voted against him; wisely, he no longer cares.

But if you do have access to the vote distribution, what is the pattern? Did you lose an internal vote or an external one? Was your denial caused by the intervention of top administrators? Beyond the numbers of votes, what is the tone of the participants? Do you have many angry partisans who claim that you came close but had your prize stolen? Or are even those who claim to have been your supporters cool to the idea of an appeal?

Power is a significant issue. Losing an internal vote may be less important than lacking the support of university administrators. A unanimous vote against you is hard to overcome; a close one may be less so. Do you have (candid) friends in high places who think you have a chance?

The same questions apply to the nuclear option: a lawsuit. If you feel wrongdoing and unfairness were at play, consulting a lawyer experienced in academic case law is a sensible course of action.

**Moving forward, restarting your career.** Suppose you decide that your best option is to restart your career somewhere else. There are real alternatives, and the news is not all bad. Just because you have been denied tenure doesn't mean you have to exit academia. Sure, you may always suffer some taint from the denial, but it need not be the stench of death. You can be reborn elsewhere.

First, some good news: Context matters, as mentioned earlier. A colleague in another field who was denied tenure described being eagerly recruited afterward. "They knew about my old department's reputation. They didn't care if I was rejected by that system." Also, if you earned your Ph.D. from a highly rated program, it will be respected by hiring committees, especially at smaller liberal arts colleges or regional state universities.

Begin your comeback by conducting an honest assessment of your CV. Administrators and search committees evaluating your application honor past achievements, but they value career trajectory even more. The CV of a person who has been denied tenure requires a key ingredient to make it palatable, even respectable: evidence of forthcoming work or grants or any major confirmation that you are on the upswing.

Now brand yourself to others as a positive colleague. As in any other business, depression, indignation, and bitterness embedded in letters of inquiry or application, or expressed in face-to-face interviews, do not add luster to your employment profile.

I have an acquaintance who, long ago, was denied tenure, and brings up the subject again and again. His unhealthy obsession has hurt his career more than did the original setback. If you can't get over your pain, learn to mask it well. Your career depends on it.

Being upbeat is not just for show, though. Bookstore shelves are full of self-help volumes that catalog successful generals, CEOs, inventors, and explorers who endured early failure before eventual triumph. If you can't stomach Oprah-esque literature, watch the "Homer & Delilah" episode of *The Simpsons* in which Homer, emboldened by a new full head of hair, becomes a motivational manager and lectures a crowd on the importance of getting beyond early stumbles. Your initial project should be writing letters of inquiry and application for open positions. Detail your achievements and describe how you would fit into the department and the job. Do not dwell on your tenure denial but do not try to cover it up, either. Explain in a sentence or two that you fell short of your goals in your previous job.

The key follow-up step is to mobilize partisans in your favor. Presumably, *someone* encouraged your tenure bid. Nothing would help your candidacy more than a letter of support from a senior professor assuring your prospective department that you would be just right for the job. (Even if a job announcement asks only for a list of references, have your champions send letters anyway.)

Perhaps the letter could say, "Dr. Phoenix was working on a big project that did not initially yield as many publications as we had hoped, but will likely do so in the future." Or it could indicate that you had put so much effort into teaching that you didn't publish enough, but that you had since learned to balance your time and your research productivity was improving.

Better yet, your advocate could point out how your perceived weaknesses at your old department might be strengths in your new one. A small liberal arts college, for example, might welcome someone who was terrific in the classroom but did not have as many publications as a high-research university demanded.

The need for internal champions is another reason you should control your level of anger and pique, or at least the expression of them. It may seem paradoxical, but even people who voted against you may want to help you leave without fuss and rancor—or a deposition. It is in the interests of the administration to have as tranquil an aftermath of tenure denial as possible. So it is reasonable, and will also heighten people's estimation of you, if you tell them forthrightly, "I accept that things didn't work out. Now I could use your help to find another job." Don't threaten; you'd be surprised how eager people will be to offer their assistance.

Deciding where to apply is a crucial decision. Do you want to try for someplace that approximates the institution you plan to leave? Do you want to switch tracks altogether?

It is hard to move horizontally after a tenure denial. But even if, for instance, you are at a top research university and want to end up at another one, you might consider finding a way station in your career. Take a good job at a regional state university that might let you regroup, earn tenure, and establish a reputation. Then, if you wish, move on. That transition is preferable to a wall of rejection from your present-day peers. Again, if you have a top-tier doctorate, you may well be welcomed back into the high-research fold with no penalty exacted for your wilderness wandering. On the other hand, you may find, as many do, that your new home turns out to fit your post-tenure-denial personality and interests, and that the golden ring you once chased has lost all its luster.

If you want to stay at the same level, look particularly for lower-ranked departments with new leadership that are trying to scale up their profiles, or older programs that have gone through many retirements and are rebuilding. A newly hired dean, director, or chair may be more willing to take a chance and be more open to hiring you.

In your cover letter and during your interview, all the standard rules of the academic search apply. Neither imperiousness nor insecurity make you a better prospect. Try to specify how you would fit into a particular program. Seek out connections—friends who have friends on the faculty. And, of course, enumerate what you are doing now and what you are planning to do, offering a glass that is half-full and bubbling up.

Finally, lessen the risks of hiring you. Ask for a shortened tenure-review process: a three-year clock, for example. If you don't work out, campus administrators know they can cut their losses quickly, and if you do prove to be a success, they can just as rapidly absorb you as a tenured (and grateful) professor.

The gratitude factor is a consequential three-P element. A humanities dean explained that she liked hiring people who were obviously very capable but had been denied tenure somewhere else, typically because of politics or personality conflicts. Her argument was, in essence, "If they're angry, that's okay as long as they're willing to channel that anger into proving to the world that their tenure denial was a mistake. In other words, they have an 'I'll show you guys' motivation. I figure, and I've seen, that they'll come here, work extra hard, be extra collegial, and be extra conscientious. And above all, they'll be loyal to the school that gave them their last chance to shine."

In short, the perfect profile of a candidate, after a tenure denial, includes the following:

- A positive attitude, displaying neither "I was too good for those fools" arrogance nor "poor pitiful me" despondency.
- A sense that, although the tenure denial was regrettable, you have put it behind you.
- Evidence that you are already planning and producing for the future.
- Internal champions who will argue that you will prosper at the new institution.

Life is unpredictable and sometimes unfair, but the tipping factor is in your favor if you can show employers that the tenure denial was a blip in your career, not an ending in itself.

You are not a loser for being shot down once, as many a downed fighter pilot can attest. You want to project the air of someone who has undergone a traumatic episode but has climbed back into the cockpit and is ready to soar—given the chance.

### You Got Tenure! Joy and Melancholy

When my own appointment letter for tenure arrived, I felt no exhilaration. People congratulated me like I was a new father, but I was moody for weeks and, at the same time, felt guilty for not being ecstatic. Earning tenure, becoming an "associate" rather than an "assistant," seemed anticlimactic.

A colleague in art history described getting tenure as "winning a race" but then said he did not actually feel victorious. One problem may have been that, unlike real racers, he was denied a victory lap, a trophy, and a cheering crowd—let alone the monetary booty accorded to Olympians or World Series victors. (At most public universities the tenure pay raise is a few thousand dollars.) The moment of our supreme achievement comes via a letter in campus mail. Maybe there are hearty congratulations at a faculty meeting, or handshakes in the hallway, or perhaps even a brief juice-and-cupcakes ceremony— hardly the stuff of Super Bowl victory bashes.

Perhaps we need to ramp up the awarding of tenure to a full-fledged party, or at least create some sort of campus ceremony during which friends and family can watch us get a plaque or a trophy. Undignified, maybe; morale boosting, absolutely.

On a philosophical level, we are all aware of the *rewards* of being a tenured professor, but the gloomy culture of the tenure track does not encourage us to dwell on them.

Sometimes outsiders are best qualified to remind us how good we have it. A few years ago I had just finished my first year of being on an eleven-month administrative calendar as an associate dean. As I was getting a haircut, my barber asked me whether I had enjoyed my summer. I answered, with some grumpiness, "Well, I had to work." She replied, "So did I." Score one for town keeping gown grounded in reality.

The best revenge against the things, events, and people that distress us is to laugh at them—generally in private. Quite a few of the most successful and happiest academics I know have healthy senses of humor and an appreciation of the absurd. There is also a careerist benefit, to wit: making your colleagues laugh—with you, not at you—goes a long way toward their deeming you a good colleague to promote and tenure.

And getting tenure is, after all, the last laugh.

Yet with victory comes responsibility. Getting P&T should also occasion some serious reflection and even strategizing about what it means, what happened, and how you can build on it.

There are two reasons why you should do so. First, it's not over. Tenure, however wrenching a process, should be the beginning—or, as Churchill put it, "the end of the beginning"—of your academic career. It would be helpful at this point to take stock of the lessons you've learned that will sustain your ascent. Such an analysis must be sober and even critical. Unfortunately, many a tenured professor presumes that attaining that status makes one sagacious in all aspects of P&T. In reality, "successful" people, institutions, and companies are not always experts in the reasons for their success. A perceptive study conducted by Alan MacCormack found that NASA did not perform postmortems of *successful* missions and thus did not learn much from them because, as he put it,

> [the space agency] fell prey to "superstitious learning"—the assumption that there is more to be gleaned from failed missions than from successful ones. In the challenging climate of space exploration, however, the difference between what makes one mission succeed and another fail can be subtle. There is no reason to believe that success indicates a flawless process while failure is the result of egregious bad practice.[1]

Indeed, it is unclear how much any of us recognize why we have succeeded in any task. So take some time for your own post-tenure review. Discuss it with peers and mentors. Ponder, reflect, and then move forward.

Second, and equally important, you have now entered the mentor class, and not just for doctoral students. You will sit on search committees and weigh the qualifications of job candidates, speculating, "Will she be able to get tenure here?" You will serve on the internal P&T committee. You will write annual reviews of assistant professors, and you will vote on their fate. You will dispense advice about how they can achieve what you have achieved. You owe it to them and to the system to be as knowledgeable and objective as possible.

## After Tenure: Your Fifty-Year Career Plan

The tenure track has often been compared elsewhere to an epic quest, a race, even a mountaineering expedition. But there is a danger in such analogies, however properly they may apply during the process. When the quest is over, the race won, and the mountain conquered (and you've gotten back to base camp), it is quite easy to forget that chronologically as well as intellectually the six years or so of seeking P&T will only be a tiny segment of your career. You have, of course, another promotion to achieve—and maybe ambitions beyond that in the form of endowed chairs or the administration (which many faculty see as a downward move!).

In fact, a few months into a new position at another university, I grasped the meaning of "long term" in academia. I was sitting in a room that served as a library for past dissertations in psychology, listening to a student defend his doctoral proposal, when a mental connection clicked. I scanned the walls of blue and black, gold-lettered, bound theses, and there it was: "Perlmutter 1952."

My father's dissertation had faded somewhat, but the typewritten, onionskin pages were still legible, and so were the names of at least two of the signatories: Roger Barker, the great University of Kansas social psychologist, and Kurt Heider, the noted sociologist. Holding that original document in my hand, with the knowledge that my father, although officially retired, was still doing research, still publishing, still teaching a class, and still *cared* after more than half a century of academic life, focused my thoughts on the importance of the long-term view in our profession.

As academics, from our earliest apprenticeships we are under considerable pressure to focus on the short term. As doctoral students, we hear the clock ticking. The best jobs go to those who begin presenting at conferences and getting published as early as possible.

We are hired on the understanding that we have either finished our dissertations or are about to. Then more fuses start to light: completing grant applications, preparing for class, grading papers, and of course publishing, publishing, publishing—all aimed at that third-year review and then at tenure evaluation.

Even after tenure, especially at research institutions, the incentive for possessing a limited horizon of thought and action is strong. We focus on producing more (and, we hope, better) publications to secure promotion to full professor, on continued grant applications, on the increasing weight of writing letters of recommendation and evaluations for students and colleagues, and on the many administrative deadlines we must meet.

But if we are granted health, luck, and sanity, the full arc of an academic career is fifty years, not sixteen weeks. As the eminent critic Cyril

Connolly argued in his *Enemies of Promise*, the creative professional could avoid early burnout and survive the "marathon of middle age" only if he understood that a career must be paced like the proverbial long-distance race, not a sprint followed by collapse and exhaustion.[2] We have to weigh what it makes sense for us to focus on in the here and now, and what is best deferred. Charles W. Haxthausen, emeritus director of the graduate program in the history of art at Williams College, mulled the choices he's made in a note to me: "Because of the demands of the administrative job I have had for the past 14 years, I did not fulfill two book contracts, but as I retire from administration and go into half-time teaching with more time for research, I am now glad that I have waited this long. I think both books will be better for having ripened in my head, and enhanced by the papers and articles I have written along the way."

Taking the half-century view of a career allows us to conceptualize our work as both a solitary venture and a group effort. As your career develops and you build alliances and partnerships with colleagues—and then with graduate students—you begin to understand how any particular area of research must satisfy the interests of not just yourself but others.

To think in the long term recognizes that our world is changing, and will change yet more. The words of Bruce Springsteen apply as much to academics today as to the steelworkers of the 1970s: "These jobs are going, boys, and they ain't coming back to your hometown." The tenured professor, while not quite an endangered species, is becoming more and more a premium position as many colleges and universities rely increasingly on visiting instructors and part-time adjuncts.

At the same time, the "unproductive" tenured professor is the bane of administrators, legislators, and fellow faculty members. Post-tenure reviews are common, and some sort of redefinition of tenure toward a mounting bar of post-tenure productivity is likely. All signs point to P&T standards rising as academics are required to prove their future potential as much as they document their past achievements. What better way to stay afloat than to think in terms of a lifetime of contributing to the creation and dissemination of knowledge? The best way to be judged well by others is to keep judging ourselves—over the long term.

Which brings us to the philosophy of success.

A number of people who fail in their academic careers by being denied promotion or tenure, or who earn tenure and then fall into an embarrassing lethargy of underachievement, do so for psychological reasons. It's not that they physically can't type, read, or gather data, or muster the energy or competence to teach and grade. It's that they lose focus, acuity, or their will to succeed. It's the mental game—as in golf—that can make or break you. And one facet of that is the danger of too much short-term thinking.

If you are focused only on immediate highs—getting a journal article accepted for publication or receiving superlative student evaluations that semester—then like an addict you will eventually experience letdown.

There is inner peace in understanding that one semester is not a referendum on whether you are a good teacher, and that one rejection letter is not the final word on your scholarship. As a senior colleague once told me, "I have been rejected by journals many times, but after a while, as I built up my CV, I realized that a rejection was not the end of anything at all." Individual humiliations and failures seem diminished, even trivial, when we lay them out in relation to a life's work.

The fifty-year career plan works only if you accept it as a metaphor and not as an actual prognosticative blueprint. In fact, many scholars do not have one long career but many different ones—a stint as a researcher, another as an administrator, or a string of periods perusing different subjects.

My father, for example, started out studying small groups as an engineer and a social psychologist. Now an emeritus professor of international business management at the University of Pennsylvania, he is writing a book on the future of human civilization. He has explored many bodies of knowledge, served in many capacities, and tells me that he still enjoys "confronting the white computer screen page as much as I looked forward to filling the blank paper in the typewriter in 1952."

Likewise, Ralph Izard, a chaired professor of mass communication at Louisiana State University in Baton Rouge, who is now in his fifth decade of scholarship, commented, "The variety of shifting foci of my work and research gives me something fresh every day. As a result, I'm more productive and happier."

The point is not to expect that for the next fifty years you will do one thing or many similar things sequentially, but that you will benefit from spending those years doing many different things. Such is the pursuit of happiness afforded to those scholars who think in the long view.

In fact, I think a final word on academic career-making belongs to the master of life quest narratives, Charles Dickens, who begins his novel *Great Expectations* with the immortal sentence, "Whether I shall turn out to be the hero of my own life, or whether that station will be held by anybody else, these pages must show." If you have beaten the odds, overcome villains, and vanquished personal demons to achieve P&T, then you *are* the hero of your own story. More important, P&T is but the first chapter of your academic life, and after completing it, rest assured that you have the right to joyfully conceive and execute the many adventures to come.

# Notes

## Introduction

1. Evelyn Hu-DeHart (2000), "Office Politics and Departmental Culture," in Mildred García, ed., *Succeeding in an Academic Career: A Guide for Faculty of Color*, 27–38 (Westport, CT: Greenwood Press), p. 27.

2. David D. Perlmutter (2000), *Policing the Media: Street Cops and Public Perceptions of Law Enforcement* (Beverly Hills, CA: Sage).

3. Franklin Silverman (2004), *Collegiality and Service for Tenure and Beyond: Acquiring a Reputation as a Team Player* (Westport, CT: Praeger).

4. S. G. Harkins and K. Szymanski (1989), "Social Loafing and Group Evaluation," *Journal of Personality and Social Psychology* 56: 934–941; J. Steven Karau and Kipling D. Williams (2000), "Understanding Individual Motivation in Groups: The Collective Effort Model," in Marlene E. Turner, ed., *Groups at Work: Theory and Research*, 113–141 (Mahwah, NJ: Lawrence Erlbaum); B. Latané, K. D. Williams, and S. Harkins (1979), "Many Hands Make Light the Work: The Causes and Consequences of Social Loafing," *Journal of Personality and Social Psychology* 37: 822–832; S. Yamaguchi, K. Okamoto, and T. Oka (1985), "Effects of Coactor's Presence: Social Loafing and Social Facilitation," *Japanese Psychological Research* 27: 215–222.

5. David D. Perlmutter and Alan D. Fletcher (1999), "Feedback That Fits: How Experienced and Naïve Students View Internships," *Journal of Advertising Education* 3(2): 9–18.

6. David D. Perlmutter (1999), *Visions of War: Picturing Warfare from the Stone Age to the Cyberage* (New York: St. Martin's Press); David D. Perlmutter (1994), "Visual Historical Methods: Problems, Prospects, Applications," *Historical Methods* 27(4): 167–184.

7. Quoted in "Mike Tyson: Boxer," *Wired*, January 2010, p. 90.

8. Quoted by Elizabeth Shores from personal interview with the American Association of University Professors (AAUP) Associate General Secretary Jordan E. Kurland. Interview conducted July 16, 2008.

9. Anthony DePalma (1991), "Rare Dismissal on California Faculty," *New York Times*, August 14, p. 17.

10. American Federation of Teachers (2009), *American Academic: The State of the Higher Education Workforce 1997–2007* (Washington, DC: American Federation of Teachers); JBL Associates, Inc. (2008), *Reversing Course: The Troubled State of Academic Staffing and a Path Forward* (Washington, DC: American Federation of Teachers).

11. American Association of University Professors (2009), "On the Brink: The Annual Report on the Economic Status of the Profession, 2008–09," aaup.org/AAUP/comm/rep/Z/ecstatreport08-09/ (accessed 3/3/10).

12. American Association of University Professors (1995), "The Status of Non-Tenure-Track Faculty," in *Policy Documents and Reports,* 8th ed., 72–81 (Washington, DC: AAUP). See also American Association of University Professors (1998), "Statement from the Conference on the Growing Use of Part-Time and Adjunct Faculty," *Academe* 84(1): 54–60.

13. Piper Fogg (2005), "A *Chronicle* Survey: What Presidents Think," *Chronicle of Higher Education,* November 4, p. A31.

14. A. E. Austin (2002), "Preparing the Next Generation of Faculty: Graduate School as Socialization to Academic Career," *Journal of Higher Education* 73(1): 94–122; R. Boice (1992), *The New Faculty Member: Supporting and Fostering Professional Development* (San Francisco: Jossey-Bass); S. Fisher (1994), *Stress in Academic Life* (Buckingham, UK: Open University Press); W. H. Gmelch, P. K. Wilke, and N. P. Lovrich (1986), "Dimensions of Stress among University Faculty: Factor Analytic Results from a National Study," *Research in Higher Education* 24(3): 266–286; Deborah Olsen and Mary Deane Sorcinelli (1992), "The Pretenure Years: A Longitudinal Perspective," in Mary Deane Sorcinelli and Anne E. Austin, eds., *Developing New and Junior Faculty,* New Directions for Teaching and Learning 50, 15–25 (San Francisco: Jossey-Bass); R. Eugene Rice, Mary Deane Sorcinelli, and Anne E. Austin (2000), *Heeding New Voices: Academic Careers for a New Generation,* New Pathways Working Paper Series, Inquiry no. 7 (Washington, DC: American Association for Higher Education); Mary Deane Sorcinelli (1992), "New and Junior Faculty Stress: Research and Responses," in Sorcinelli and Austin, eds., *Developing New and Junior Faculty,* 27–37; Sorcinelli and Austin, *Developing New and Junior Faculty;* Mary Deane Sorcinelli (1994), "Effective Approaches to New Faculty Development," *Journal of Counseling and Development* 72(5): 474–479; E. J. Thorsen (1996), "Stress in Academe: What Bothers Professors?" *Higher Education* 31(4): 471–489.

15. Xenia Hadjioannou, Nancy Rankie Shelton, Danling Fu, and Jiraporn Dhanarattigannon (2007), "The Road to a Doctoral Degree: Co-travelers through a Perilous Passage," *College Student Journal* 41: 160–177; B. Lovitts and C. Nelson (2000), "The Hidden Crisis in Graduate Education: Attrition from Ph.D. Programs,"

*Academe* 86: 44–50; D. Shannon, D. Twale, and M. Moore (1998), "TA Teaching Effectiveness: The Impact of Training and Teaching Experience," *Journal of Higher Education* 69: 440–454; J. Weidman, D. Twale, and E. Stein (2001), *Socialization of Graduate and Professional Students in Higher Education* (San Francisco: Jossey-Bass); D. L. Wiseman (1997), "Patterns of Mentoring: Weaving Teacher Educators' Career Stories," in C. A. Mullen, C. K. Boettcher, and D. S. Adoue, eds., *Breaking the Circle of One: Redefining Mentorship in the Lives and Writings of Educators,* 189–199 (New York: Peter Lang).

16. Thomas Hallock (2004), "Joy! Rapture! I've Got a Brain!" *Journal of Scholarly Publishing* 36: 27–33.

17. S. Finkel Kolker, S. G. Olswang, and N. She (1994), "Childbirth, Tenure, and Promotion for Women Faculty," *Review of Higher Education* 17: 259–270; R. Wilson (1999), "Timing Is Everything: Academe's Annual Baby Boom: Female Professors Say They Feel Pressure to Plan Childbirth for the Summer," *Chronicle of Higher Education,* June 25, pp. A13–A15.

18. Vicki Rosser (2005), "Measuring the Change in Faculty Perceptions over Time: An Examination of Their Worklife and Satisfaction," *Research in Higher Education* 46(27): 81–107.

19. U.S. Department of Education, National Center for Education Statistics (2001), *Digest of Education Statistics,* nces.ed.gov/pubs2002/digest2001/tables/dt274.asp/ (accessed 3/3/10).

20. U.S. Department of Education, National Center for Education Statistics (2005), "Table 224. Employees in Degree-Granting Institutions, by Race/Ethnicity, Residency Status, Sex, Employment Status, Control and Type of Institution, and Primary Occupation: Fall 2003," nces.ed.gov/programs/digest/d05/tables/dt05_224.asp?referrer=report (accessed 3/3/10).

21. For the ratio of men to women, see "Characteristics of Recipients of Earned Doctorates, 2006" (2007), *Chronicle of Higher Education,* December 7, chronicle.com/article/Characteristics-of-Recipients/47071/ (accessed 3/3/10).

22. S. Acker and G. Feuerverger (1996), "Doing Good and Feeling Bad: The Work of Women University Teachers," *Cambridge Journal of Education* 26(3): 401–422; D. E. Davis and H. S. Astin (1990), "Life Cycle, Career Patterns and Gender Stratification in Academe: Breaking Myths and Exposing Truths," in S. S. Lie and V. E. O'Leary, eds., *Storming the Tower: Women in the Academic World,* 89–107 (New York: Nichols/GP Publishing); S. K. Finkel and S. G. Olswang (1996), "Child Rearing as a Career Impediment to Women Assistant Professors," *Review of Higher Education* 19(2): 123–139; M. F. Fox (1995), "Women in Scientific Careers," in S. Jasanoff, G. E. Markel, J. C. Peterson, and T. Pinch, eds., *Handbook of Science and Technology Studies,* 205–224 (Thousand Oaks,

CA: Sage); L. Grant, I. Kennelly, and K. B. Ward (2000), "Revisiting the Gender, Marriage, and Parenthood Puzzle in Scientific Careers," *Women's Studies Quarterly* 1&2: 62–85; K. McElrath (1992), "Gender, Career Disruption and Academic Rewards," *Journal of Higher Education* 63(3): 269–281; L. Wolf-Wendel and K. Ward (2003), "Future Prospects for Women Faculty: Negotiating Work and Family," in B. Ropers-Huilman, ed., *Gendered Futures in Higher Education: Critical Perspectives for Change,* 111–134 (Albany: State University of New York Press).

23. Janice Neuleib (1997), "Special Challenges Facing Women in Personnel Reviews," in Richard C. Gebhardt, Barbara Genelle, and Smith Gebhardt, eds., *Scholarship, Promotion, and Tenure in Composition Studies,* 129–135 (Mahwah, NJ: Lawrence Erlbaum), p. 131.

## 1. The Doctorate and the Career Track

1. M. J. Finkelstein (1984), *The American Academic Profession: A Synthesis of Social Scientific Inquiry since World War II* (Columbus: Ohio State University).

2. Melanie R. Benson (2009), "At What Cost?" *Chronicle of Higher Education,* December 4, pp. B10–11. See also "For Black Doctoral Students, an Education in Debt" (2007), *Chronicle of Higher Education,* April 6, chronicle.com/article/Black-PhDs-Face-High-Levels/47413/ (accessed 3/3/10).

3. The "early" and "switch colleges to get promoted" options were not on my radar back then, although I would use them myself to shave a few years off that track. Also, some universities have seniority grades for full professors, so, for example, a top rank would be "Professor III."

4. Joanne Cooper and Dannelle Stevens, eds. (2002), *Tenure in the Sacred Grove: Issues and Strategies for Women and Minority Faculty* (Albany: State University of New York Press); Joann Moody (2004), *Faculty Diversity: Problems and Solutions* (New York: Routledge Falmer); Viernes Turner, Caroline Sotello, and Samuel L. Myers (2000), *Faculty of Color in Academe: Bittersweet Success* (Boston: Allyn and Bacon).

5. E. T. Pascarella and P. Terenzini (1978), "The Relation of Students' Precollege Characteristics and Freshman Year Experience to Voluntary Attrition," *Research in Higher Education* 9(4): 347–366; E. T. Pascarella and P. Terenzini (1980), "Predicting Freshman Persistence and Voluntary Dropout Decisions from a Theoretical Model," *Journal of Higher Education* 51(1): 60–75; E. T. Pascarella and P. Terenzini (1983), "Path Analytic Validation of Tinto's Model," *Journal of Educational Psychology* 75(2): 215–226.

6. L. J. Horn (1998), *Stopouts or Stayouts? Undergraduates Who Leave College in Their First Year*, NCES 1999-087 (Washington, DC: U.S. Government Printing Office); T. T. Ishitani (2003), "A Longitudinal Approach to Assessing Attrition Behavior among First-Generation Students: Time-Varying Effects of Pre-College Characteristics," *Research in Higher Education* 44(4): 433–449; A. M. Nunez and S. Cuccaro-Alamin (1998), *First-Generation Students: Undergraduates Whose Parent Never Enrolled in Postsecondary Education*, NCES 1999-082 (Washington, DC: U.S. Government Printing Office).

7. See the review in Kul B. Rai and John W. Critzer (2000), *Affirmative Action and the University: Race, Ethnicity, and Gender in Higher Education Employment* (Lincoln: University of Nebraska Press).

8. Benson, "At What Cost?" See also "For Black Doctoral Students."

9. Scott Jaschik (2007), "Hope on Ph.D. Attrition Rates—Except in Humanities," *Inside Higher Ed*, December 7, insidehighered.com/news/2007/12/07/doctoral (accessed 3/3/10).

10. B. Lovitts and C. Nelson (2000), "The Hidden Crisis in Graduate Education: Attrition from Ph.D. Programs," *Academe* 86: 44–50, p. 45.

11. H. Angelique, K. Kyle, and E. Taylor (2002), "Mentors and Muses: New Strategies for Academic Success," *Innovative Higher Education* 26: 195–209.

12. Linda Cooley and Jo Lewkowicz (2003), *Dissertation Writing in Practice: Turning Ideas into Text* (Hong Kong: Hong Kong University Press); James E. Mauch and Namgi Park (2003), *Guide to the Successful Thesis and Dissertation: A Handbook for Students and Faculty* (New York: Marcel Dekker); Judith M. Meloy (1994), *Writing the Qualitative Dissertation: Understanding by Doing* (Mahwah, NJ: Lawrence Erlbaum); R. Murray Thomas and Dale L. Brubaker (2001), *Avoiding Thesis and Dissertation Pitfalls: 61 Cases of Problems and Solutions* (Westport, CT: Bergin and Garvey).

13. David D. Perlmutter and Lance Porter (2005), "Thinking beyond the Dissertation," *Chronicle of Higher Education*, December 16, pp. C1, C4.

14. David Heenan (2002), *Double Lives: Crafting Your Life of Work and Passion for Untold Success Stories of Extraordinary Achievement* (Yarmouth, ME: Intercultural Press).

15. Michael Polanyi (1967), *The Tacit Dimension* (New York: Anchor Books); Eugene Herrigel (1981/1953), *Zen in the Art of Archery* (New York: Random House).

16. Robert Boice (2000), *Advice for New Faculty Members: Nihil Nimus* (Boston: Allyn and Bacon); C. M. Golde (2000), "Should I Stay or Should I Go? Student Descriptions of the Doctoral Attrition Process," *Review of Higher Education* 23(2):

199–227; M. Nettles and J. Johnson (1987), "Race, Sex, and Other Factors as Determinants of College Students' Socialization," *Journal of College Student Personnel* 28(6): 512–524; M. Nettles (1990), "Success in Doctoral Programs: Experiences of Minority and White Students," *American Journal of Education* 98: 494–522.

17. D. Carter, C. Pearson, and D. Shavlik (1988), "Double Jeopardy: Women of Color in Higher Education," *Educational Record* 68(4): 98–103; L. W. Debord and S. M. Millner (1993), "Educational Experiences of African American Graduate Students on a Traditionally White Campus," *Equity and Excellence in Education* 26(1): 60–71; Evelynn M. Ellis (2001), "The Impact of Race and Gender on Graduate School Socialization, Satisfaction with Doctoral Study and Commitment to Degree Completion," *Western Journal of Black Studies* 25(1): 30; J. E. Girves and V. Wemmerus (1988), "Developing Models of Graduate Student Degree Progress," *Journal of Higher Education* 59(2): 163–198; Nettles, "Success in Doctoral Programs"; Robert E. Nolan (1999), "Helping the Doctoral Student Navigate the Maze from Beginning to End," *Journal of Continuing Higher Education* 48(3): 27–32; V. Tinto (1993), *Leaving College: The Causes and Cures of Student Attrition* (Chicago: University of Chicago Press); C. S. V. Turner and J. R. Thompson (1993), "Socializing Women Doctoral Students: Minority and Majority Experiences," *Review of Higher Education* 16: 355–370.

18. Ellis, "Impact of Race."

19. Leonard Valverde (1980), "Promotion Socialization: The Informal Process in Large Urban Districts and Its Adverse Effects on Non-Whites and Women," *Journal of Educational Equity and Leadership* 1(1): 36–46.

20. Horn, *Stopouts or Stayouts?*; Ishitani, "A Longitudinal Approach"; Nunez and Cuccaro-Alamin, *First-Generation Students.*

21. J. E. Blackwell (1981), *Mainstreaming Outsiders: The Production of African American Professionals* (New York: Harper and Row); R. T. Hartnett and J. Katz (1977), "The Education of Graduate Students," *Journal of Higher Education* 48(6): 646–664.

22. Piper Fogg (2008), "When Generations Collide," *Chronicle of Higher Education,* July 18, p. B18; B. Tulgan and C. A. Martin (2001), *Managing Generation Y: Global Citizens Born in the Late Seventies and Early Eighties* (Amherst, MA: HRD Press), pp. 1–102.

23. Xenia Hadjioannou, Nancy Rankie Shelton, Danling Fu, and Jiraporn Dhanarattigannon (2007), "The Road to a Doctoral Degree: Co-travelers through a Perilous Passage," *College Student Journal* 41(1): 160–177; B. Lovitts and C. Nelson (2000), "The Hidden Crisis in Graduate Education: Attrition from Ph.D. Programs," *Academe* 86: 44–50; D. Shannon, D. Twale, and M. Moore (1998), "TA Teaching Effectiveness: The Impact of Training and Teaching Experience,"

*Journal of Higher Education* 69: 440–454; J. Weidman, D. Twale, and E. Stein (2001), *Socialization of Graduate and Professional Students in Higher Education* (San Francisco: Jossey-Bass).

**2. The Academic Job Search**

1. David D. Perlmutter (2010), "Professionalize Promotion and Tenure," *Chronicle of Higher Education*, February 18, chronicle.com/article/Professionalize -Promotion-a/64223/.

2. Rhetoric/Composition 2009 Wikia, "Rhetoric/Composition 2008–2009," academicjobs.wikia.com/wiki/Rhetoric/Composition_2009 (accessed 3/4/10).

3. "Knowing Your Competition," *Chronicle of Higher Education*, January 4, 2010, chronicle.com/blogPost/Knowing-Your-Competition/19506/ (accessed 3/4/10).

4. Anonymous poster, The venting page Wikia, post dated 2010-03-26, http:// academicjobs.wikia.com/wiki/The_venting_page.

5. See the research on status of programs: Val Burris (2004), "The Academic Caste System: Prestige Hierarchies in PhD Exchange Networks," *American Sociological Review* 69: 239–264; Lee Harvey (2008), "Rankings of Higher Education Institutions: A Critical Review," *Quality in Higher Education* 14: 187–207; Debra Hevenstone (2008), "Academic Employment Networks and Departmental Prestige," in Thomas N. Friemel, ed., *Why Context Matters: Applications of Social Network Analysis*, 119–140 (Orlando, FL: VS Verlag); Bruce Keith (1999), "The Institutional Context of Departmental Prestige in American Higher Education," *American Educational Research Journal* 36: 409–445; Bruce Keith and Nicholas Babchuk (1998), "The Quest for Institutional Recognition: A Longitudinal Analysis of Scholarly Productivity and Academic Prestige among Sociology Departments," *Social Forces* 76: 1495–1533; Pamela Paxton and Kenneth A. Bollen (2003), "Perceived Quality and Methodology in Graduate Department Ratings: Sociology, Political Science, and Economics," *Sociology of Education* 76: 71–88; David L. Weakliem, Gordon Gauchat, and Bradley R. E. Wright (2008), "Sociological Stratification: The Prestige of Graduate Departments of Sociology, 1965– 2007" (paper presented at the Annual Meeting of the American Sociological Association, Boston, July 31), allacademic.com/meta/p241378_index.html (accessed 3/4/10).

6. David DiRamio, Ryan Theroux, and Anthony J. Guarino (2009), "Faculty Hiring at Top-Ranked Higher Education Administration Programs: An Examination Using Social Network Analysis," *Innovative Higher Education* 34: 149–159.

7. Yale University, American Studies Program (2009), "Publications: Directory of Graduate Programs," theasa.net/publications/grad_programs/item/american_ studies_program18 (accessed 3/4/10).

8. Weakliem, Gauchat, and Wright, "Sociological Stratification."

9. Burris, "Academic Caste System"; David Jacobs (2004), "Ascription or Productivity? The Determinants of Departmental Success in the NRC Quality Ratings," *Social Science Research* 33: 183–186; Keith, "Institutional Context"; Keith and Babchuk, "Quest"; Paxton and Bollen, "Perceived Quality."

### 3. Colleagues and Academic Cultures

1. Susanna Calkins and Matthew R. Kelley (2005), "Mentoring and the Faculty-TA Relationship: Faculty Perceptions and Practices," *Mentoring and Tutoring: Partnership in Learning* 13(2): 259–280; Janie M. Harden Fritz (2002), "How Do I Dislike Thee? Let Me Count the Ways: Constructing Impressions of Troublesome Others at Work," *Management Communication Quarterly* 15(3): 410–438; James C. Hearn and Melissa S. Anderson (2002), "Conflict in Academic Departments: An Analysis of Disputes over Faculty Promotion and Tenure," *Research in Higher Education* 43(5): 503–529.

2. Major works on racism in the academy include Philip G. Altbach, Kofi Lomotey, and Clark Kerr (1991), *The Racial Crisis in American Higher Education* (Albany: State University of New York Press); Kul B. Rai and John W. Critzer (2000), *Affirmative Action and the University: Race, Ethnicity, and Gender in Higher Education Employment* (Lincoln: University of Nebraska Press).

3. Wendy R. Boswell, Jan Tichy, and John W. Boudreau (2005), "The Relationship between Employee Job Change and Job Satisfaction: The Honeymoon-Hangover Effect," *Journal of Applied Psychology* 90(5): 882–892.

4. Eyal Ophira, Clifford Nassb, and Anthony D. Wagner (2009), "Cognitive Control in Media Multitaskers," *Proceedings of the National Academy of Sciences of the U.S.A.* 106: 15583–15587. See also G. B. Armstrong and L. Chung (2000), "Background Television and Reading Memory in Context: Assessing TV Interference and Facilitative Context Effects on Encoding versus Retrieval Processes," *Communications Research* 27: 327–352; David B. Buller (1986), "Distraction during Persuasive Communication: A Meta-analytic Review," *Communication Monographs* 53: 91–114; K. Foerde, B. J. Knowlton, and R. A. Poldrack (2006), "Modulation of Competing Memory Systems by Distraction," *Proceedings of the National Academy of Sciences of the U.S.A.* 103: 11778–11783; A. Furnham and A. Bradley (1997), "Music While You Work: The Differential Distraction of Background Music on

the Cognitive Test Performance of Introverts and Extraverts," *Applied Cognitive Psychology* 11: 445–455. See a popular review in Fenella Saunders (2009), "Multitasking to Distraction," *American Scientist* 97(6): 455.

5. Oili-Helena Ylijoki and Hans Mäntylä (2003), "Conflicting Time Perspectives in Academic Work," *Time and Society* 12: 55–78; Loren W. Tauer, Harold Fried, and William Fry (2007), "Measuring Efficiencies of Academic Departments within a College," *Education Economics* 15: 473–489.

6. Jonathan B. Spira and David M. Goldes (2007), *Information Overload: We Have Met the Enemy and He Is Us* (New York: Basex), p. 17.

7. See parameters of research on time management in the workplace, including academia: Christopher D. B. Burt and Darryl K. Forsyth (2001), "Relationships between Supervisor Behavior, Family Support and Perceived Time Management Ability," *New Zealand Journal of Psychology* 30: 4–8; Hugh Kearns and Maria Gardiner (2007), "Is It Time Well Spent? The Relationship between Time Management Behaviours, Perceived Effectiveness and Work-Related Morale and Distress in a University Context," *Higher Education Research and Development* 26: 235–247; Linda J. Sax, Linda Serra Hagedorn, Marisol Arredondo, and Frank A. Dicrisi III (2002), "Faculty Research Productivity: Exploring the Role of Gender and Family-Related Factors," *Research in Higher Education* 43: 423–446; Tauer, Fried, and Fry, "Measuring Efficiencies"; Ylijoki and Mäntylä, "Conflicting Time Perspectives."

8. Kearns and Gardiner, "Is It Time Well Spent?"

9. U.S. Federal Aviation Administration (2000), *Ten Ways to Help Prevent Runway Incursions*, FAA poster presentation, http://findarticles.com/p/articles/mi_m0IBT/is_9_63/ai_n27440522; Institute for Safe Medication Practices (2005), "Sterile Cockpit," *ISMP Medication Safety Alert,* March 24, ismp.org/Newsletters/acutecare/articles/20050324_3.asp (accessed 3/9/10); Ruth King (2002), "Runway Incursions, Reducing the Risk," *Flight Safety Australia* January–February: 24–29; E. L. Wiener (1985), "Beyond the Sterile Cockpit," *Human Factors* 37: 75–90.

10. There is strong research from medical practice about how interruptions decrease the quality of doctor-patient relations. See, for example, Myez Jiwa, Robert McKinley, Carolyn O'Shea, and Hayley Arnet (2009), "Investigating the Impact of Extraneous Distractions on Consultations in General Practice: Lessons Learned," *BMC Medical Research Methodology* 9(8): 1–6; J. Urkin, A. Elhayany, P. Ben-Hemo, and A. Abdelgani (2002), "Interruptions during Consultations—Harmful to Both Patients and Physicians," *Harefuah* 141: 349–352, 409, 410.

11. Seneca (1932), *Moral Essays,* vol. 2, trans. John W. Basore (Cambridge, MA: Harvard University Press), p. 243.

12. W. Felps, T. R. Mitchell, and E. Byington (2006), "How, When, and Why Bad Apples Spoil the Barrel: Negative Group Members and Dysfunctional Groups," *Research in Organizational Behavior* 27: 181–230.

13. Peter Blau (1964), *Exchange and Power in Social Life* (New York: Wiley); Gary Chan (2008), "The Relevance and Value of Confucianism in Contemporary Business Ethics," *Journal of Business Ethics* 77: 347–360; Nicholas Economides, Giuseppe Lopomo, and Glenn Woroch (2009), "Strategic Commitments and the Principle of Reciprocity in Interconnection Pricing," in Gary Madden and Russel Cooper, eds., *The Economics of Digital Markets*, 62–99 (London: Edward Elgar); C. M. Korsgaard (1996), *Creating the Kingdom of Ends* (Cambridge, UK: Cambridge University Press); Roger C. Mayer, James H. Davis, and F. David Schoorman (1995), "An Integrative Model of Organizational Trust," *Academy of Management Review* 20: 709–734; W. Vendekerckhove and M. S. R. Commers (2004), "Whistle Blowing and Rational Loyalty," *Journal of Business Ethics* 53: 225–233; Sandra A. Wawrytko (1982), "Confucius and Kant: The Ethics of Respect," *Philosophy East and West* 32: 237–258.

14. Confucius (1938), *The Analects,* vol. 6, trans. Arthur Waley (New York: Random House), chapter 28.

### 4. The Balancing Act—Self, Family, and Tenure

1. For comparison, see Larry H. Ludlow and Rose M. Alvarez-Salvat (2001), "Spillover in the Academy: Marriage Stability and Faculty Evaluations," *Journal of Personnel Evaluation* in *Education* 15(2): 111–119.

2. Christopher D. B. Burt and Darryl K. Forsyth (2001), "Relationships between Supervisor Behavior, Family Support and Perceived Time Management Ability," *New Zealand Journal of Psychology* 30: 4–8.

3. David A. Heenan (2002), *Double Lives: Crafting Your Life of Work and Passion for Untold Success* (Palo Alto, CA: Davies-Black).

### 5. Student Relations

1. Allen Sanderson, Voon Chin Phua, and David Perda (2000), *The American Faculty Poll* (Chicago: National Opinion Research Center). Their statistics, which reflect a nationally representative sample of full-time college and university faculty members, were derived from a telephone survey poll of 1,511 undergraduate educators. About their degree of satisfaction with their current position, 39.2 percent

of faculty were very satisfied; 51.9 percent were satisfied; 6.9 percent were not very satisfied; and 1.3 percent were not at all satisfied. Faculty identified their nine primary stressors as:

50%: Student preparation and commitment
47%: Workload
41%: Lack of institutional support
35%: Intra-departmental strains
31%: Inter-departmental strains
31%: Family responsibilities
30%: Inability to obtain research grants
15%: Physical or health problems
13%: Personal finances

2. Mary Morris Heiberger and Julia Miller Vick (2001), *The Academic Job Search Handbook* (Philadelphia: University of Pennsylvania Press), pp. 42–46.

3. Ode Ogede, ed. (2002), *Teacher Commentary on Student Papers: Conventions, Beliefs, Practices* (Westport, CT: Bergin and Garvey).

4. Many teaching texts talk about office hours. For an excellent overview of the office hour as part of the new class prep, see the chapter on "Preparing Your Courses" in Sandra Goss Lucas and Douglas A. Bernstein (2002), *Teaching Psychology: A Step by Step Guide* (Mahwah, NJ: Lawrence Erlbaum).

5. For guidance on door etiquette, see David B. Kelly (2008), "Students' Perspectives on Materials Posted on Faculty Office Doors," *College Student Journal* 42(4): 1009–1014.

6. Gypsy M. Denzine and Steven Pulos (2000), "College Students' Perceptions of Faculty Approachability," *Educational Research Quarterly* 24(1): 56–66; M. Lamport (1993), "Student-Faculty Informal Interaction and the Effect on College Student Outcomes: A Review of the Literature," *Adolescence* 28: 971–990.

### 6. Steps to Tenure and Promotion and Beyond

1. Alan MacCormack (2004), "Management Lessons from Mars," *Harvard Business Review* 82(5): 18–19.

2. Cyril Connolly (1983), *Enemies of Promise* (New York: Persea Books).

# Acknowledgments

*Promotion and Tenure Confidential* is the product of almost a decade of conversations and ruminations. The former included hundreds of e-mail, forum, telephone, and face-to-face exchanges with academics and graduate students. I thank them all, but particular gratitude is extended to those who read the manuscript (or portions of it) and commented on it: Hazel Dicken-Garcia, Roland Racevskis, Ted Gutsche, the reviewers and editorial board of Harvard University Press, and my editors Jeanne Ferris and Denise Magner at the *Chronicle of Higher Education*. Supreme appreciation goes to my patient and probably long-suffering editor Elizabeth Knoll, who suggested the idea of the book and nursed it to its fulfillment. Finally, as expressed in the dedication, this manuscript, like everything I've produced in my professional life, owes its existence to the support and insight of my wife, Christie.

# Index